how to be an
entrepreneur

Books that make you better

Books that make you better. That make you *be* better, *do* better, *feel* better. Whether you want to upgrade your personal skills or change your job, whether you want to improve your managerial style, become a more powerful communicator, or be stimulated and inspired as you work.

Prentice Hall Business is leading the field with a new breed of skills, careers and development books. Books that are a cut above the mainstream – in topic, content and delivery – with an edge and verve that will make you better, with less effort.

Books that are as sharp and smart as you are.

Prentice Hall Business.
We work harder – so you don't have to.

For more details on products, and to contact us, visit
www.pearsoned.co.uk

Steve Parks

how to be an entrepreneur
The Six Secrets of Self-Made Success

PEARSON
Prentice Hall
BUSINESS

Harlow, England • London • New York • Boston • San Francisco • Toronto
Sydney • Tokyo • Singapore • Hong Kong • Seoul • Taipei • New Delhi
Cape Town • Madrid • Mexico City • Amsterdam • Munich • Paris • Milan

PEARSON EDUCATION LIMITED

Edinburgh Gate
Harlow CM20 2JE
Tel: +44 (0)1279 623623
Fax: +44 (0)1279 431059
Website: www.pearsoned.co.uk

First published in Great Britain in 2006

ISBN-13: 978-0-273-70829-2
ISBN-10: 0-273-70829-5

British Library Cataloguing-in-Publication Data
A catalogue record for this book is available from the British Library

Library of Congress Cataloging-in-Publication Data
A catalog record for this book is available from the Library of Congress

10 9 8 7 6 5 4 3 2 1
10 09 08 07 06

Typeset in 11pt Minion by 70
Printed and bound in Great Britain by Bell & Bain Ltd, Glasgow

The publisher's policy is to use paper manufactured from sustainable forests.

Contents

Acknowledgements

My thanks to all the entrepreneurs who have spoken so openly to me about their work and who have shared their advice, experiences, and techniques.

In particular I would like to thank those who do not normally talk to journalists or writers – but who were so candid and frank with me.

I would also like to express my appreciation for the support provided to me by everyone at my publisher (but especially Rachael Stock who nursed this project, as all my books), my girlfriend, my family, my friends – and especially my colleagues in my businesses – during the research and writing of *How to be an Entrepreneur*.

Introduction

I am often asked by people to define what makes an 'entrepreneur'.

My first response is: 'An entrepreneur is someone starting or growing a business who distinguishes themselves with their ambition and achievement.'

The simplicity of this often surprises people. They expect me to say something that limits the kind of people who could be considered entrepreneurs, and therefore that they are a special breed who are in some way different from everyone else from birth. Perhaps: 'You can only be an entrepreneur if your father died while you were young, you're dyslexic, you dropped out of your deprived inner-city school at 14 having started your first business selling stuff in the playground, etc, etc.'

Not true. In fact, it's not even close.

STEREOTYPES

Please leave any preconceived ideas you have of entrepreneurs at the door. They're plain wrong.

Entrepreneurs are just ordinary people like you and me. They come from all sorts of backgrounds – but where they differ is in the attitudes and skills they develop from this starting point. I strongly believe that these entrepreneurial attitudes and skills can be learned, and that is what this book is about.

Remember that newspapers and TV programmes only feature a certain kind of entrepreneur because they are the ones who want to take part in programmes or have their picture in the papers. There are many hundreds of thousands more who prefer to remain private or even anonymous.

Anonymity doesn't mean they are any less successful. Fame does not equal success in business. In fact, it can often be quite the opposite.

There are no rules on who can be an entrepreneur. You are not barred from this club if you have a degree or if you don't. Entrepreneurs can be male or female, of all sorts of creeds and colours. Entrepreneurs can come from rich or poor backgrounds.

You do not have to have had a tough childhood in a poor family, and have left school at 16. In fact, entrepreneurs are more likely to have come from well-off families (like Richard Branson, despite what he might seem to suggest in his PR!). But there are plenty of examples of people who started with nothing. Your social background and current wealth is irrelevant.

You do not have to be 'wild and wacky' with loads of 'crazy' ideas. I know ex-accountants and computer geeks who have built very successful businesses.

You do not have to be young and trendy. Most entrepreneurs start their businesses in their 30's or 40's, but others start in their 50's or 60's, and some start in their 20's – and a few have even started in their teens. It's never too early, and never too late.

You do not have to be in a trendy, busy, bustling city – statistically most entrepreneurs actually start their businesses in rural areas.

The image of the stereotypical entrepreneur is wrong.

And here's the secret of all secrets. For any other job you need to persuade someone to recruit you and give you that job title. To become an entrepreneur, you only need to prove to yourself that you can do it, and give yourself the job title. It's a self-recruiting profession.

Whatever your background you can become an entrepreneur – if you want to do it enough, and if you put in the work.

YOU

If you do want to build a new business, grow an existing business, or are just fascinated by the entrepreneurs who do build and grow successful businesses, this book is for you.

You may be daunted by the challenges ahead on your chosen path, and looking to learn about how others have tackled them. You may have encountered some of these problems already and be looking for inspiration to help you succeed.

You may be harbouring a desire to strike out on your own in business, and are searching for information about what's involved.

This book draws on the experiences of a wide range of highly successful entrepreneurs to bring you an insight into how they have built such thriving businesses.

I strongly believe that we can all become much more successful simply by learning from those who have gone before us. We're not going to learn academic theory, or an accountant's or bank manager's view on how to start a business – we're going to learn from real entrepreneurs who have made millions, and even billions, from actually starting and running businesses.

By providing this insight into the behaviour of real entrepreneurs I hope this book can help you to tread an easier path to entrepreneurship, avoiding some of the most common mistakes.

THE PROBLEM

About 30,000 new businesses launch in the UK every month.

Less than half of them will still be operating in 3 years' time.

To me, that's a problem.

That failure is awful for those involved – the founders, their staff, their families, their investors and their suppliers. It hurts their wallets, their self-confidence, and their pride. It's highly stressful – and it's heart breaking.

So why do so many small businesses fail, while at the same time some are so enormously successful?

Most of the time it's down to the founder having made a series of fairly simple mistakes. Mistakes that have been made by thousands of entrepreneurs before.

We need to break this cycle and start learning from the entrepreneurs who have preceded us. What did they do right? What did they do wrong?

THE DIFFERENCE BETWEEN A SMALL BUSINESS OWNER AND AN ENTREPRENEUR

As well as the businesses that fail, there are many others that just chug along and never really achieve the dreams of their founder. The owner of the business is stuck in the hamster wheel – if they try to get out it soon stops spinning. They have to keep running away in there. These operations are always just 'small businesses' rather than entrepreneurial businesses.

Real entrepreneurship is about building something that is bigger than just the founder. It's about creating a lasting and successful business – that will still be lasting and successful even when the entrepreneur has moved onto a new project (I would say the beach, but let's be honest, it's nearly always a new project with real entrepreneurs!).

One of the tangible differences between small business owners who never achieve great success and highly successful entrepreneurs who are rapidly growing their businesses, is that the former are running around doing the everyday work while entrepreneurs put their energy into building the business itself.

For a small business owner, each day is a new series of battles to keep up with the demands and problems of customers, the bank, investors, staff and suppliers. They never seem to find the time to develop the company itself, so that things become more stable and the business can grow.

Entrepreneurs employ others to deal with the work – their job is to build the teams and systems that make up the business, not to actually do whatever it is the company does.

They develop a company that doesn't rely on them at all to do the real work for customers. If they fall under the proverbial bus tomorrow the business would live on. It would miss their charisma and inspiration, but it would be capable of continuing, unaffected by their loss. Customers would still be served in the same way, the work would still get done, and the company would still prosper. Their intention is to build an organization that doesn't need them.

Small business owners shape their businesses around them so that the company absolutely depends on them being there 16 hours a day and working like crazy – not just in the start-up phase, but forever. They find it difficult to let go of the day-to-day work and responsibility. They find it difficult to delegate and trust others. They don't like the idea of their company not needing them anymore.

Think of your business like a child. It can't depend on you forever. At some point it has to grow up, move away and stand on its own two feet. You have to let this happen – and what's more, you have to spend its formative years preparing it for this moment. You must equip it with the attitudes, skills and experience to survive in the big wide world without you.

THE NEED FOR *HOW TO BE AN ENTREPRENEUR*

Until now all information and training for entrepreneurs has been about details, like doing the tax return, doing the accounts, preparing a business plan, meeting the bank manager, dealing with employment legislation, and so on. Hard facts – stuff that keeps you in the hamster wheel.

But the things that I have found distinguish successful entrepreneurs from those whose businesses never really take off are actually the 'soft' skills such as developing the right attitudes, motivating and managing people, building networks, developing ideas, and so on. These are not only the vital distinguishing factors in being successful, but also the hardest for most of us to get to grips with. They will help you break out of the hamster wheel and build a business that can survive and prosper on its own.

The business failure statistics clearly show that the current training and support for budding entrepreneurs isn't working. We need to spend more time and effort looking at what successful entrepreneurs think and do, and helping the next generation to develop those attitudes and skills.

We need to identify what works and what doesn't, and pass that experience on to other people who are starting businesses.

HOW I CAME TO WRITE THIS BOOK

Ten years ago I left my job as a journalist with BBC Radio and started building my own group of companies. I wasn't satisfied with the way the mainstream media reported on business, and saw an opportunity to deliver specialist news and information to executives and entrepreneurs.

My organization, The Red Group, has grown rapidly since then and is now the world's leading publisher of business audio, exporting CDs and downloadable programmes to dozens of countries.

Among the projects my companies run is a monthly audio magazine for business leaders, and in my work for this I have been able to undertake in-depth interviews with many top entrepreneurs.

These interviews sowed the seed for this book, and I've since taken the time to meet and interview many other entrepreneurs – sometimes just over a pint.

Stories and examples from these people are included throughout *How to be an Entrepreneur* – although anonymously in some cases. Because of that anonymity we get the true story – a real insight into real entrepreneurship – rather than just PR puff that is included in so many profiles of entrepreneurs.

Having so much contact with entrepreneurs has helped me identify the challenges that they face, including those I've seen even the very successful ones struggling with. To help us tackle these problems I've drawn on the thinking of some of the world's top business minds to inspire solutions. These people include management guru Tom Peters, personal development guru Stephen Covey, small business guru Michael Gerber, personal development guru Steve McDermott, personal effectiveness coach David Allen and business thinker Jim Collins.

Many of their ideas were originally targeted at the leaders of large companies, but I find that they can be adapted to be equally suited to entrepreneurs.

THE SIX SECRETS OF SELF-MADE SUCCESS

Through my interviews and research I found six key areas in which entrepreneurs show particular strengths – and that these strengths have a clear effect on the success of their business.

These six areas are:

1. **Attitude**. Entrepreneurs have certain attitudes that help them achieve more than other people. Some of these they're aware of, and they stress the importance of, while others are almost subconscious. These core beliefs and characteristics are instrumental in their success, and the most important distinguishing factor between these successful people and others.

2. **Opportunity**. Entrepreneurs are practised at finding or creating opportunities – at all stages in the development of their businesses. The techniques they use can be clearly identified, and used by others.

3. **Focus**. In amongst all the flood of work involved in starting and growing a business, entrepreneurs have a laser-like focus on what's important. They use techniques – some naturally, some by design – that help them and the whole business to focus on the critical success factors.

4. **Talent**. These highly successful people are constantly seeking to learn and to develop their own talents, but they are also expert at releasing and harnessing the talents of others – and aiming the effort towards a specific goal.

5. **Building**. Instead of running around doing the day-to-day work, successful entrepreneurs are building their businesses. They do this by carefully building a brand, building a team, building resources, building systems and building in security.

6. Communication. Entrepreneurs are great communicators. That isn't just about talking, it's also about listening. The best create whole communities around their businesses.

This book is divided up into chapters to match these six secrets.

Everybody is different, so everybody is going to take different things from this book. What's certain is that nobody is going to follow everything in here to the letter.

It's designed to inspire and inform – not to instruct. Read it with an eye for ideas you can lift out and apply, and tools that seem to fit your needs. It will be worth reading even if you only try out a few things and find them useful.

I recommend revisiting *How to be an Entrepreneur* on a regular basis to see if any other ideas might be worth using as your situation changes and you face different challenges.

JOINING THE COMMUNITY

The whole philosophy behind this book is that entrepreneurs learn best from other entrepreneurs.

To that end I've created an online community at **www.flyingstartups.com** to support readers of this book and my other entrepreneurial books. The site includes blogs, forums and other resources to help entrepreneurs to help each other. I'm also a regular visitor on the site and help out where I can.

You can also join the Institute of Entrepreneurs to network with and learn from others. This is a new membership organization run by entrepreneurs, for entrepreneurs – and I'm one of the founders: **www.instituteofentrepreneurs.co.uk.**

ALL FOR ONE, AND ONE FOR ALL!

So, as we embark on our journey of entrepreneurial discovery, let's remember that although we're all individuals pursuing our independent dreams we'll all face similar challenges, and enjoy similar successes.

Let's share our knowledge and experience, let's collaborate and co-operate, and let's spur each other on to achieve more than we ever thought was possible.

All for one, and one for all!

CHAPTER ONE
The first secret: Attitude

Being successful in anything is largely about your attitude. I'm not talking simply about the need to be 'positive' – you can find lots of other books to help you with that. We're going to look at a whole range of attitudes of mind and beliefs that successful entrepreneurs have.

I know that there are going to be some people reading this who think that working on your attitude is not a vital part of being successful. They believe that accounting skills or other technical expertise are more important. But those people are plain wrong.

Having a successful business is not about technical skill. Richard Branson doesn't have a pilot's licence or any experience in maintaining aeroplanes. He doesn't know how to prepare a set of company accounts, but has that held him back at all? He can easily hire people with technical skills.

Having a successful business is not about qualifications. There's an endless list of very rich and successful entrepreneurs with no certificates past school level (this doesn't mean that not having any qualifications is actually an advantage by the way, just that they have nothing to do with business success).

Having a successful business is not about having lots of money. Sure, it makes it easier to start *a* company, but it doesn't help to make a *successful* business.

Having a successful organization *is* about having the right set of attitudes. These attitudes guide you in the key decisions of your business. They keep you going when times are tough. They are the difference between those who fail and those who succeed. Your attitudes are what your customers will pick up subconsciously and use in their decision to buy from you, and buy from you again. Your attitude will be the difference between starting *a* business and starting a *successful* business.

The challenge for you is that many of these attitudes and beliefs contradict each other. A normal reaction is that this is impossible, you have to choose one or the other – however the key is to have both, but in balance. Think of the Chinese idea of yin and yang – two opposing things that are in balance. They have this philosophy in martial arts, fortune telling and even cooking (think sweet and sour). In the West we generally want to be definitely one thing or the other, but that's not the most effective way to be.

This section is also going to bust a few myths about the attitudes, beliefs and characteristics of the really successful entrepreneurs; the ones you see on TV or in the newspapers are not representative. Many really successful entrepreneurs actually shun the media limelight. I know one rich entrepreneur who hired an expensive PR agency for the sole purpose of politely declining any interview requests, and another very, very successful entrepreneur who offered the compiler of *The Sunday Times* Rich List £20,000 if they would leave him *off* the list. Believe me, these two are much more successful than 99 per cent of the entrepreneurs you read about or see on TV, and they have very different attitudes.

This section of the book is going to be the part that rubs some people up the wrong way – especially the media. They demand that business books give clear, simple answers that fit a nice stereotype. They want all entrepreneurs to be fun-loving, ego-driven adventurers – but unfortunately it's a bit more complicated than that. Entrepreneurs have very complicated mixtures of attitudes and beliefs, and this is my attempt to document the reality rather than the myth. The good news about this is that even if you aren't a wild and wacky ego-driven stereotype, you can be an entrepreneur!

So, with the understanding that these attitudes are going to seem atypical and contradictory, I challenge you to open your mind, and try them out for size. Imagine they are clothes you are thinking of buying. Put them on, and see how they feel for a bit. Thinking of attitudes in this way can be a powerful tool to help you develop an entrepreneurial mindset.

SIMPLE ATTITUDES

It's going to get complicated and contradictory in a moment so let's start with a few simple warm-ups before I start giving you brain-ache.

These first six attitudes are simple, straightforward, golden rules. Successful entrepreneurs use these like the guiding beam from a light-house. If they trust in them even when the going is really tough, they know they will make it through.

Entrepreneurs are responsible, principled, open, passionate, versatile and resilient.

Responsible

I don't mean that entrepreneurs avoid drinking too much and are always in bed by 9pm – I mean responsible in the sense that they take total responsibility for what happens in their lives and their businesses.

Most people try to shirk responsibility. Do you ever hear people say, 'They should do something about that', when they see a problem? Who are 'they'? For these people it's always someone else who ought to be making something happen.

With entrepreneurs the focus is on taking responsibility for making things happen. This is how they change the world. They see a problem and say, '*I* could do something about that'.

And if things don't work out they don't shirk the blame either.

Managers in big companies are always finding someone else to blame for things. Every year they announce their financial results and say, 'Sales were down this year because of . . . the weather being too hot . . . the weather being too cold . . . the World Cup . . .'. There's always some excuse, rather than stating, 'I didn't manage people well enough and give them the resources to do the job', 'We had a poor product in comparison to our competitors' or 'We weren't very good at selling'.

For example, business organizations are constantly complaining that the biggest problem in business is 'red tape' – the rules and regulations set by government. Lazy journalists picked this up as an easy story, and you'll constantly see variations on the theme in the papers. Are these organizations really saying that their members' biggest problems aren't in their management teams, or the amount of sales they make, or their cost base? Are they running the perfect company, doing things perfectly every time?

Of course they're not. But they want to pass the blame for any problems they have to someone else before they take responsibility themselves.

Insider Knowledge

I was a member of the Institute of Directors for a while, but they won't let you into their building unless you wear a tie (something I very rarely do). This is one of the rules and regulations they insist members abide by! Who's guilty of needless regulation there – government or business? I haven't seen a law passed yet that says I have to wear a tie – I think this is because governments are a bit busy passing legislation to stop people getting killed, alleviating poverty, and providing education and health services. Let's stop trying to blame the governments, or Europe, or any other people – and let's focus on taking responsibility for making our business better. Let's sell more so we can afford good professional advisers to help us deal with the regulations, so we can focus on the important stuff.

I should also stress that I have no party political allegiance. All governments charge taxes, and all governments make rules, regardless of the party in power. Politicians are in a profession that can never win with the public or the business community. Corporate managers are busy either sucking up to them, or complaining about them – real entrepreneurs just ignore them (unless they spot an opportunity!) and get on with the work.

By shirking the responsibility these business leaders are giving away the power to avoid the same problem in the future. If it's completely up to someone else then what can they possibly do about it?

Entrepreneurs keep this power by knowing that it is down to them, and only them, to do what needs to be done. This doesn't mean they don't delegate – quite the opposite – but they retain the overall responsibility. If things go wrong, it is because of some action they have done wrongly – or most often, some action they haven't done at all.

Because they have the power of responsibility they can sit back, work out what they did wrong, and change their approach the next time around. They don't look for excuses or a scapegoat, they look for things that they can improve. That gives them a huge advantage over competitors who don't take responsibility.

It's also a strangely liberating feeling. I remember the motivational guru Steve McDermott, who has been a big influence on me, arrived late to a meeting and said, 'Sorry I'm late. I didn't set off on time'.

Other people would have blamed traffic, parking or anything else but their own actions. Everyone in the meeting was visibly surprised by his honesty – and couldn't help but smile and forgive him. I tried this myself later and it felt great. I didn't feel bad about making an excuse, and it made me realize the real reason why I was late more often than I would like, and I started setting off earlier for future meetings. I took the power to change the situation by taking responsibility.

Tool

How to practice being responsible

1. Look for problems everywhere you go. In each case make yourself think about what *you* could do to fix them.

2. If something goes wrong in your business or your life, large or small, then take a moment to reflect on what *you* could have done differently to avoid it, and therefore what *you* will do in the future to avoid it.

3. Actively listen out for yourself blaming other people or 'them', and tell yourself off!

4. When you're about to give an excuse for something, stop yourself and be honest – take the responsibility.

Principled

Would you turn down £1m if the sole condition attached to it was that you did something that you didn't believe was right – not criminal or even slightly illegal, just not the right thing to do?

Insider Knowledge

I know an entrepreneur who did just that. He'd built up a business that had been doing pretty well, but had hit a few problems. He needed to raise extra finance for the company. After going through the fundraising process he was left with two offers on the table. In the first he would sell the business for a very small token sum and walk away, but the new owners would invest in it and grow it, retaining all the current staff. In the second he would be paid £1m, and the new owner would close the business, make all the staff redundant, and simply use the brand-name and products elsewhere.

What would you do?

He was a real entrepreneur and he had principles. He sacrificed personal gain for what he thought was the right thing to do. He showed loyalty to the staff who had helped him build the business from nothing. He walked away with nothing after ten years of work.

That is what being principled is about – having beliefs in what is right and wrong that are so strong they override all temptation.

Some entrepreneurs do flout this golden rule, and they can get to be very successful – for a while. But they have a tendency to fall flat on their faces eventually, even if that takes decades. False success doesn't last, and it doesn't make people happy.

Insider Knowledge

I know of one person who calls himself an entrepreneur who did make a lot of money, but he lied and cheated to get it. He believes that business is a game to be played fast and loose, and you have to do whatever it takes to earn the money. If someone else suffers along the way, that's their problem. He made quite a few million pounds when he sold his business – and began to lead the millionaire lifestyle – but has never been able to replicate his success. I constantly hear venture capitalists, bankers, suppliers and others complain about him and they refuse to work with him again. That has made life very difficult for him when it comes to building new ventures, and those he has tried have failed. His money has leaked away very quickly.

Meanwhile my friend who walked away from his business with nothing has built up a couple more highly successful businesses – and the process was made so much easier by people who wanted to do him favours because they respect his principled approach. People like him and want to see him succeed. His fortunes are very definitely on the rise.

Real entrepreneurs have principles, and they stick to them even when it hurts.

They're rewarded for this by the system of karma which means that the things you do for or to other people, good or bad, will be repaid to you eventually in some way.

Tool

How to practice being principled

1. Decide what your personal principles are. Write them down. What lines will you refuse to cross?

2. Carry this list with you and when faced with a moral dilemma – however small – take a few moments to consult it. Stick to the principles you have decided on, even if it hurts.

Opportunities can come up almost every day in small ways. Will you gossip about someone behind their back? Will you take the biggest portion of chocolate cake, or pass it to someone else? Will you let another motorist out into the traffic during rush hour?

As well as defining the 'line in the sand' that you will not cross in difficult moral decisions, principles should also be positive beliefs that you take a conscious decision to act on.

Insider Knowledge

One entrepreneur in San Francisco decided that one of the principles of his company was to give something back to the community and spread 'niceness' without seeking credit. They didn't just wait for other people to bring them opportunities to put this principle into action. He gave all his staff prepaid tickets for the toll bridge, and asked them to also pay for the motorist behind them on their way to work each day. Can you imagine the bemused smile on these motorists' faces when the toll booth attendant told them the person in front had paid for them? What a nice way to start the day, for both the giver and the receiver.

What can you do to pro-actively put your principles into action? Don't just wait for the moral dilemmas to challenge you in order to show the world what you're made of.

Open

One of the findings that surprised and impressed me about the real entrepreneurs was that they were very open.

By this I mean that they were open by being receptive to new people and ideas, and that they were willing to be open by sharing information and contacts.

Let's look first at the idea of being open by being receptive. In a big company the chief executive may say, 'My door is always open', but you've generally got to get past security guards, a receptionist, swipe card systems and a secretary before you get there. Only people they already know, or know they want to know, can get any kind of communication in there, whether that's by phone, email, letter or in person.

That means that CEOs are very closed off from the outside world. They don't know what the real views of real customers are, they don't know what problems people have when using their products or services, and they don't know what new innovations might be possible. In fact they will only ever know what they already know, or what the people close to them think they may want to hear in order to be rewarded with promotion (or avoid the sack).

Insider Knowledge

James Dyson found this out the hard way when he tried pitching the idea for his dual cyclone vacuum cleaner to Hoover, the market leader. The underlings there turned him away and told him, 'If there was a better vacuum cleaner to be made, we'd have made it'. The CEO will never have got to hear about it until it was too late.

Meanwhile, entrepreneurs realize that they constantly need to be receiving stimulus from the outside world in order to be the best they can be. They love meeting new people, they love hearing new ideas. They go to events specifically to expose themselves to new people and listen to what they have to say. They make themselves available on the phone, and they read their post and emails themselves.

Insider Knowledge

One very well known entrepreneur told me that he often answers the general public telephone number for his business, which really surprises the person on the other end of the line, but he gets to find out very interesting things about what customers, suppliers and others really think.

When I worked for BBC Radio, the receptionist wanted to take a day off but the manager hadn't been able to arrange any cover. I and a couple of other journalists volunteered to do a couple of hours each on reception to solve the problem. I not only found out that being on reception is quite hard – working the switchboard and keeping track of callers on hold was tough, let alone dealing with the volume of calls or all the people coming in and out of the building – but I also found out so much about what listeners thought and wanted. In doing the normal daily work I didn't get nearly the same feedback from listeners as I did that day.

Inside their business, entrepreneurs make sure that they get out and about to meet people, and find out how things work. They have their ear close to the ground and can spot early signs of trouble, be prepared for an increase in demand, or be aware of a change in customer needs. They are less likely to be caught off guard.

Entrepreneurs are open to learning from the past. They read lots of biographies of successful entrepreneurs, they go to hear them speak at events, they read magazine articles about them, and they read books like this – all in an attempt to try and acquire knowledge from the past mistakes or successes of other people, rather than having to go through these things the hard way on their own. They also learn from the past in their business – but without letting it consume too much of their time or attention. After each sale they'll have a quick analysis of 'Why did we win or lose? What could we do differently next time?', and then they'll move on – simply learning the lesson without trying to blame anyone.

They're also open to ideas. When someone pitches an idea to them they're interested, and listen. They're excited about the new rather than fearful of it.

They actively seek out new ideas and information. They read magazines, books and newspapers. They listen to audio CDs (this isn't just a plug for my business – I found a surprising number of entrepreneurs learn in this way because they can listen in their cars, and often using my competitors' products too. Grrr!). They go to events and training courses. They search the Internet. They build up a network of contacts and mentors who they can ask for advice, information and ideas.

In short, they make sure that they are open to receiving.

But they are also open in terms of giving. For a start, they are happy to pass on their experiences and advice. So many successful entrepreneurs were happy to be open and chat to me in the research for this book, and many also speak at events, mentor other businesses, and pass on their knowledge in other ways.

This openness comes from the fact that they don't believe that there is only a limited amount of success out there, and only the few people who battle for it can claim this elusive prize. They believe that success is unlimited and as many people as work for it can achieve it. So helping someone else doesn't dent you own chances.

In fact helping someone else achieve success can often mean that you get helped out in the future – remember the idea of karma?

If you ask a successful entrepreneur for information, advice or contacts they will usually help you out without asking for anything in return, simply because they are open. What would happen if someone were to ask you for the same?

Finally, they are open to the truth and open with it, whereas ego-driven businesspeople put up a smokescreen of lies and half-truths to make themselves and their organization look good. Real entrepreneurs tell it how it is. I found this to be particularly true with their teams. They would let people know honestly how the company was doing and what the challenges were, they were open about how much money they were getting and how much work they were doing, and they were open and honest about what they thought of other people and their work.

Insider Knowledge

I think a great example of an entrepreneur who is open and honest with his team is the chef Gordon Ramsay. He has built up a fantastic business of high-class restaurants, but he has also earned a reputation for being rude and abrasive. When you dig below the media hype though you find out that his staff absolutely worship him, and he has a very loyal, dedicated team who stay with him for far, far longer than is usual in the restaurant industry. Is that the sign of someone who is rude and abrasive? No.

They appreciate his openness and honesty. The people who don't perform are criticized strongly and clearly, the people who do are respected and praised. His is a business in which workers prosper and shirkers perish. The workers love this sense of fairness, and the recognition of their work.

I highly recommend catching an episode or two of Ramsay's 'Kitchen Nightmares' TV programme, and you will see his people skills at work. Watch and learn – you can use those skills in your business. He has a clear set of principles about what is acceptable and what is required. If someone is not meeting those principles because of lack of skill he shows them how; if they are not meeting them because of an attitude problem he comes down on them like a ton of bricks and explains exactly what he expects of them; and if they still fail to respect this then they're out on their ear. If they raise their game and are clearly making an effort then he recognizes and rewards that. He is totally open and honest about how he feels about the person and their work. He doesn't dodge the issue or store up resentment. He tells it like it is.

Tool

How to practice being open

1. Be more open about how you feel about people and their work. This can seem awkward at first, so start gently and develop this more over time.

2. Be sure to listen to people's ideas and comments.

3. Answer your company's main telephone number from time to time – or do half a day on reception.

4. Make sure you regularly get out to spend some time on the front line in your business.

Passionate

People often say that entrepreneurs are full of confidence, but it actually goes beyond this – they're full of passion.

We're talking here about a passion that drives you through good times and bad. A passion that rubs off onto your team and your customers. A passion for what you do. A passion for where you are going.

This passion will enable you to prosper where others fail, to keep going when you might otherwise give up.

Life will throw all sorts of challenges at you and your business, and if you aren't really inspired and motivated about what you're doing it will be easy to become dispirited, and even to give up.

But besides keeping you going in difficult times, this passion will inspire your team to achieve more than would otherwise be possible. People love to be led by someone who is passionate about the work.

Customers also seem to be tuned in to whether the management of a business, and the business as a whole, are passionate about their work, their products or services, and their customers – and they respond extremely well to this. Think of companies you come into contact with. Perhaps there are some – even just something like a sandwich shop – that you are loyal to because they are passionate about what they do.

People will be more loyal, and pay more, if you are passionate. This is an area where entrepreneurs have an instant advantage over corporate businesses where the leader is so far removed from the front line that the passion just can't seep through the layers of middle managers.

Being passionate means that perfection matters to you. Your products and services must be of perfect quality, delivered perfectly on time and perfectly to budget. 'But that's impossible!' some may cry. That doesn't mean you should aim lower. A passionate entrepreneur won't settle for anything less than the best.

If you speak to the teams that work with really successful entrepreneurs the word 'perfectionist' comes up very regularly. They know that the entrepreneur is passionate about perfection, and they strive to deliver.

They don't think about cutting corners and hoping the boss won't notice. They know the boss will spot it instantly, and that the boss cares.

But you have to have the same standard with your own work. Hold yourself to higher standards than anyone else, and do the work that is needed to deliver them. Practice and refine what it is you need to do. Study and learn – not necessarily through traditional routes but perhaps from mentors or colleagues. Constantly improve the way you do things.

Be passionate.

Tool

How to practice being passionate

1. This is the one thing that's difficult to practice – passion needs to be genuine.

2. If you're not passionate about what you do, you can't pretend – you need to change your business to do something you are passionate about.

3. I know entrepreneurs who are absolutely passionate about the waste disposal industry – so you don't have to be in a glamorous line of work!

Versatile

Although entrepreneurs are absolutely passionate and full of confidence about their ideas and plans, they always have a Plan B. They know that nothing ever goes to plan, and they are ready for that.

You might be surprised to know that if you were to take a flight from London to New York the plane would be off course for 95 per cent of the flight. This isn't because there's anything wrong with the aircraft or the pilot, but because external conditions have their effect and mean that it just isn't possible to fly the perfectly straight lines that are on the flight plan. Instead, the pilot, or autopilot, is constantly taking corrective action to ensure that the plane still reaches the final destination. The resulting journey would look more like a wavy line going from London to New York, fairly near the planned course, but rarely in exactly the same place.

Running a business is very similar. You'll develop the business plan, but as you put it into action external forces will push you off course. Customers won't behave as expected, suppliers will have problems, competitors may present challenges, and so on. If you don't monitor your position against the plan and take corrective action then you could end up at a completely different destination.

Inexperienced entrepreneurs start to panic when they find that things aren't going to plan. They try to bury their head in the sand and stop looking at the information that suggests they are off course. They pretend to themselves and everyone else that things will work out somehow, but they don't actively do anything. I've been there and remember what that was like. It's only in later years that I realized what my successful entrepreneur friends did and began to replicate it.

They had absolute confidence in Plan A – but they always had a Plan B. They managed to hold this strange dichotomy in their head that Plan A was brilliant and would work perfectly – but that nothing ever goes to plan so we'd better be ready to switch to a carefully thought out Plan B.

Sometimes Plan B wouldn't be thought through very formally – but the entrepreneurs concerned had got so used to coming up with Plan B's (and C's and D's) that their mind could instantly develop a clever alternative – like a river finding the next easiest course if it gets blocked at any point. This takes practice though, so you'd better start off by planning your Plan B's in advance: eventually backup options will become second nature to you and you can 'wing it' a bit more.

Entrepreneurs also have subconscious systems to support this versatility – they build up and maintain great contacts, meaning they always know someone who can help; they keep up to date with industry news and gossip, so they get earlier warning of potential problems; and they have helped many people whenever they can, so there are always people available who are willing to return a favour.

But versatility isn't always just about responding to problems – it's also about embracing change as a great thing rather than constantly looking for the safety of the known. The best solution today may not be the same as the best solution yesterday. Every day brings the possibility of new ideas, new opportunities, and new ways to improve what you do. You should be the first to embrace these – don't wait until competitors have spotted them too.

Tool

How to practice being versatile

1. For the next thing you plan, make yourself develop a Plan B in parallel with Plan A. What are the things that could stop Plan A working, and what would you do if they happened? That's Plan B.

2. Start enjoying change. Do small things like taking a different route to work each day. Move your desk to a different place in the office for a while. Get lunch from somewhere new. Changing small stuff like this really does help improve your versatility when it comes to the big stuff.

Resilient

The most common piece of advice that the entrepreneurs I interviewed wanted to pass on to others was: 'Never, ever, give up.'

Every single one of them had been through at least one terrible experience where they had thought their business was about to go under. They had hit some huge obstacle they hadn't expected, they hadn't made enough sales, a major customer had pulled out, a major customer hadn't paid, they ran out of cash – these were the most common experiences – but there were a variety of heart-stopping moments.

At any one of those times the entrepreneurs concerned could have joined the statistics of the more than 50 per cent of start-up businesses that fail within the first three years. The option to give up was there – and not only seemed the easiest thing to do, it seemed the only thing to do.

But they didn't give up. They drew on some inner well of determination and resilience and took the hardest route – they carried on and solved the problems.

The entrepreneurs who survive are the ones who don't give up.

Resilience is also about the day to day. Running a business isn't easy. People will tell you it's a crazy idea, that you don't have what it takes, that you don't stand a chance against the big competitors or any one of a hundred other demotivating things. You have to become resilient and keep your motivation in the face of this.

You also need resilience to make any sales in your business. Research has shown that the average sale involves the customer saying 'no' five times before they say 'yes'. So, so many salespeople give up on the third or fourth 'no', when they are most of the way to 'yes'. You need to be resilient and learn to love 'no' because it is on the way to 'yes'.

But resilience can go wrong and become arrogance, pig-headedness or other negative attributes. Your resilience should not annoy other people, it should impress them. Be sensitive to the way they react to it. Don't be a bull in a china shop.

Tool

How to practice being resilient

1. The best way to develop resilience is in the sales environment. If you haven't yet started your own business perhaps you could ask your current boss to be given an opportunity to work in sales for a while? They'll be amazed and probably pleased.

2. If you do already run your own business, get out there and meet customers, try selling, get used to the doubts, the rejections, and bounce back. Learn to be resilient.

COMPLEX ATTITUDES

So far we've looked at the simple attitudes of being: responsible, principled, open, passionate, versatile and resilient. These attitudes produce straightforward ways of behaving.

But there are some attitudes that entrepreneurs display that seem to be opposite to each other. It's like the Chinese concept of yin and yang – two opposing forces that are in balance.

Small/big

The difference between small business owners whose companies fail or just tick along and entrepreneurs whose businesses grow to become hugely successful, is largely down to their mindset regarding the size of their business from the outset.

Most people set out at the start to run a small business. But a few entrepreneurs in every thousand set out to run a big business – even if it's only a one-man-band at the beginning. They are starting a big business that just happens to be at an early stage.

So what does it mean to be a 'big business at an early stage'? It means running your business so you have most of the advantages and benefits that (good) large companies have, while still retaining the advantages of small companies. This not only helps you to create a business with firmer foundations, but it also helps you to avoid the growing pains that companies face as they expand.

In this book I'm suggesting that you adopt the attitude of an entrepreneur running a big company at an early stage. Your company is a small-BIG company – bringing the planning and controls that large companies have developed to your small and agile young business to give it greater stability and a head start.

Don't panic!

I want to stress that just because we are aiming to take the best bits about big business and bring them to your company, it doesn't mean you have to lose any of the advantages of being small.

Big companies are simply too slow, too boring and too set in their ways to compete effectively with small business through any other routes than price-cutting, throwing huge amounts of money at traditional advertising or using strong-arm tactics. But they have developed and tested structures, systems, procedures and tools over many years as the result of problems and innovations. They are well funded, and control their money carefully.

Small businesses are nimble and creative. They are closer to their customers and their suppliers, building solid and lasting relationships. They can respond quickly to opportunities or threats. They can do everything cheaper, faster or more effectively than big businesses. But they can be disorganized, financially unsound and rely too heavily on the founder.

Imagine the advantage you can achieve in the marketplace by combining the advantages of your company's small size with the planning, management and other skills and tools from successful big companies.

But, becoming a small-BIG business does not mean that you are committing your company to actually becoming a big business one day. You can use these ideas and tools whatever the size of your organization.

There's nothing to say that every entrepreneur has to create a £100m business that they float on the stock exchange or sell to a multinational company. I know many highly successful entrepreneurs who restrict the growth of their company in terms of people and turnover because they have reached what they see as the perfect size. They're among the happiest entrepreneurs I know. There are others who regret growing their business too much, because at a certain stage they had to bring in the money men (they do always seem to be men) – and that changed the operation completely.

You can be a small-BIG business at any size and stage. You decide how big you want to be in terms of sales turnover or staff numbers. It is okay to stop growing if you want to – you're the boss. Being a small-BIG business just means that your small business will be better run, more profitable, more fun and less stress. Does that sound okay?

So our first contradiction for you to adopt as part of your attitude to your business is that you are a small business, but a big business: you're a big business at an early stage.

Later in this book, in the 'Building' chapter, we're going to look at the kind of systems and procedures you can put in place to help you become a small-BIG business.

Language and attitude

The language you use has a big impact on the attitude you have to something. It helps create the right mindset. We won't go into all the scientific research that backs this up right now, you'll just have to trust me. (If you don't trust me, get a book on NLP (Neuro-Linguistic Programming) or search for it on the web.)

Throughout this book I will talk in language that is most commonly associated with bigger public companies. I mention shareholders, directors, board meetings and so on. That doesn't mean you have to be running a big company in order to put these into effect, it just means that you need to think like one.

If you are a sole trader or part of a partnership you should still think of yourself as having a number of distinct relationships with the business. You are an owner, so think of yourself as a shareholder. You're also, at various times, taking the roles of director, manager, and maybe even salesperson, human resources manager and tea-maker too!

If you do run a limited company then make sure you don't fall into the trap of running it with the language of a sole trader, forgetting that you have different legal relationships with the company. You are a shareholder, a director and an employee (probably a manager).

It is really beneficial to think of your business as something separate from you, and to use this language to split out your different relationships with it; otherwise you just get dragged into being the manager, and forget about being the shareholder or the director.

A shareholder (in a private company) has a much more long-term view. They're looking for a return on their investment over a number of years. They're looking for financial rewards that will allow them to fund the lifestyle they dream of – their version of success.

A director has a more mid-term view. They're looking to satisfy the shareholders, and planning the mid-term strategy that will allow them to achieve that long-term result. They decide the overall direction of the business. Will the company start making product X, or delivering service Y? Is product A proving difficult to earn enough profit on, and should it be dropped in the next year if it doesn't turn around? What are your competitors up to?

A manager has to worry about the day-to-day running of the business. Who's off sick today? Will the order for so-and-so be dispatched on time? Etc, etc. They get so wrapped up in problems that it's hard to see anything else.

If you just think of yourself in one role, then the chances are you will get dragged into the management role, as anything that's short term seems more urgent. You end up fire-fighting, when you should be working to prevent fires in the first place.

You have to put work in to each of your positions, and it's actually the shareholder and director roles that will allow you to contribute the most value to your business. Eventually you shouldn't be a manager at all. How unlikely does that sound right now? Trust me.

Do you see how helpful it can be to treat your business as something separate from you, and to split up your different relationships with it? So even if you are a sole trader or partnership, think of yourself as a shareholder.

So whatever language I use in this book don't think it counts you out. You have to step up to it and act as if you are a big business at an early stage. Remember you are running a small-BIG business.

Risk/certainty

Here's the next yin and yang for you to balance, and the first big myth to explode about entrepreneurs. Contrary to everything you've heard, successful entrepreneurs do not take wild risks.

Entrepreneurship is about assessing risk, then finding clever ways to reduce it until you can move nearer to certainty that the idea will work. Only when the balance between risk and certainty has been achieved do real entrepreneurs go with an idea.

You won't find many successful entrepreneurs who regularly play the lottery, even in the past, before they were successful. They know the odds are long and they know that they can't control anything in order to better the odds, so what's the point? On the other hand you may have seen stories in the news that a couple of entrepreneurs have formed companies to pioneer public space travel for tourism – just a few years after the Space Shuttle disaster – which seems much more risky than entering the lottery! But these guys are no fools, and they are reducing the risks as much as they can by hiring the best talent, doing incredibly thorough research, understanding their target market, and in many other ways.

That's an extreme example, but the same is true of much more standard businesses. The founders assess where the risks are, then they try to reduce those risks by hiring people with the right experience, investing in specialist equipment, commissioning detailed research, doing careful planning, etc.

You're never going to be able to eliminate all risks to bring conditions nearer to certainty, and you then have to balance these with other, separate certainties. So, for example, there may be a risk that customers will be slower to understand a new product than expected, so the successful entrepreneur first plans a programme of education, designs the marketing very carefully and tests it on the target audience. Then, to counter any remaining risk, they ensure that there is the certainty of enough funding behind the company to cope in case sales revenues don't come in as quickly as anticipated.

To be a really successful entrepreneur when it comes to risk you need to:

1. Assess the risks.

2. Be open and honest about the potential risks within the business.

3. Plan and take action to minimize those risks in advance.

4. Assess any remaining risks.

5. Have an 'emergency plan' in place in case those risks become reality.

6. Revisit your risk planning regularly.

Your attitude needs to be that risk is fine when it's understood, minimized, and balanced with certainty.

Rich/poor

Entrepreneurs are often very tight with cash. They know what a valuable resource it is and that it shouldn't be frittered away on wasteful things. They despair at, while taking full advantage of, big companies whose managers have to stress about spending all their remaining budget at the end of the year in order to keep the same budget, and therefore power-base, next year.

The money in the entrepreneur's business is their money. The less that is spent the more they can invest in making the business more secure for the future and achieving their lifestyle ambitions.

At the same time they know that customers like to buy from companies that seem successful. If a customer thinks that a company is too new they will wait to see how it goes. If customers think that a company might be in trouble they will run to the competitors.

You need to project a successful image from the very start, and maintain it even when the going gets tough.

A cautionary word: this does not mean going out to buy flashy cars, as so many male entrepreneurs seem intent on doing. Remember that you have to balance being 'rich' in image with your 'poor' attitude. And that applies even if there's a healthy bank balance. So even when you're a millionaire, do you really need a top of the range BMW or will that Volvo be much more suitable to the task? And how about getting it secondhand?

This balance of rich/poor will affect a lot of the decisions you make about the bigger costs in your business, such as selecting premises.

Insider Knowledge

I once advised an entrepreneur who was starting a consultancy business. No one was ever going to visit her offices as she always worked on the clients' site, but she was considering getting some offices just so that it looked better on her stationery, as her clients were going to be fairly large companies who wouldn't normally deal with one-man-bands. Actual offices would have cost lots of money, and a virtual office setup (where they receive your post and calls and forward them) would still have required outlay. I advised her to simply embellish her address a little. She had her study in the spare room at 168 Park Avenue, so her address became 'Ms Example, Senior Consultant, Example Consultants, 3rd Floor, 168 Park Avenue, Example Town'. Now that's a small bit of hype, adding '3rd Floor', but it instantly says to people that it's not a residential address, and the postie will stick it through the letterbox for number 168 just the same.

At the very start of my business I operated from my rented flat. The address was 'Flat 28, Lister Court'. I adapted this to become 'Suite 28, Lister Court' to make it sound like part of a business centre. A small change, but I think commissioning editors at the BBC might have had a different view on my company if they knew it operated out of a small flat – despite the radio programmes and features being exactly the same!

If you hear enough stories from entrepreneurs about their early years you'll hear many ideas about balancing the rich and poor attitudes. One pair I met even went as far as having their office filled with fictional characters that they did the voices for on the phone – people in the accounts department, the receptionist, the warehouse and so on – even though there were only two of them working there. A bit of a risky and energy-consuming embellishment, and taking it a bit far I think, but probably lots of fun!

Respectful/cheeky

A lot of people who try to start their own business but who struggle, or have a short-term success followed by a failure, often have the characteristic of being arrogant. They mistake the typical entrepreneurial confidence with having a big ego and a lack of respect for other people. They end up annoying people, and needlessly building extra barriers for themselves. I know people who are mild-mannered and always willing to help anybody who now refuses to work with certain businesspeople simply because of their lack of respect.

Successful entrepreneurs respect the people who work for them, they respect their customers, they respect their shareholders – and here's the surprise – they respect their competitors.

Respect is demonstrated by being aware of people's work and ideas, being willing to give them time and attention, and taking them seriously. If you follow the advice in Chapter 4 on Talent then you'll hire people who are much cleverer than you at certain things, so give them the respect they deserve, and let them play an important role in developing your business. The same is true of other people you have dealings with.

But at the same time, entrepreneurs know that a bit of cheek is a valuable tool. You never get anything unless you ask. Why not use a bit of cheek to ask your main customer if they will pay upfront for the next few jobs to help you recruit an extra member of staff to work on their account? Why not use a bit of cheek to go and chat to a very senior member of staff at a major potential client when you're next at a trade event? If you don't ask you'll never get.

The difference is that cheekiness is something that happens between people who, in reality, respect each other. Think of your personal relationships: who might you ask a cheeky favour of? Your best friends, the people you respect the most. So you have to balance your cheek with respect, otherwise you will come across as arrogant and selfish.

When it comes to competitors, successful entrepreneurs still balance respect and cheek. A great example of this is easyJet and Ryanair, the low cost airlines. They are always having cheeky jibes at the other's expense, but you can be certain that they respect each other. The management at each airline will follow the actions of the other carefully, they will have strategy meetings trying to work out the other's next move and, as has become apparent from complaints to the regulators, they each pore over the other's advertisements, examining each special offer or claim of superiority. It's like two world-class boxers in the ring, respectful of their opponent and their skills, but looking for every opportunity to slip a cheeky jab through the defences.

Luck/strategy

One of the most common complaints from highly successful entrepreneurs is about a comment people make to them all the time: 'You're so lucky.'

It drives them nuts because they know that those people define luck as something that just falls into your lap, happening entirely by chance or sometimes because you went to the right school, had the right friends, etc.

Entrepreneurs do believe in and thrive on luck, but their definition of it is of something positive that happens because you opened your mind to it happening, made sure you created as many opportunities as possible for it to happen, reacted quickly and expertly when the opportunity arose, and persisted until the result was achieved.[1]

You can make entrepreneur-style luck happen by:

1. **Directing your mind to what you are seeking.** Have you ever had the experience where you've decided to buy a particular type of car – say a silver Audi A3 – then you suddenly see this type of car everywhere. Where did they all come from? Well, they were there all along but you filtered them out because they weren't important to you. As soon as you had set your mind to thinking about them you began to notice them. The same is true of opportunities. If you can direct your mind to a certain type of opportunity you will spot it more easily when it happens. You'll start to notice things people mention in passing, articles in magazines or other things you would have missed in the past. You'll be amazed how many 'lucky' things start presenting themselves once you start looking for them.

2. **Creating as many opportunities as possible for finding what you want.** This means getting out and meeting as many people as possible, reading newspapers, magazines and Internet message boards, attending trade events, and so on. It also means being

---

1 For more detail on how successful people view luck compared with unsuccessful people, dip into one of these books: *The Luck Factor*, Professor Richard Wiseman, Arrow, 2004; *The Book of Luck*, Ann Watson and Heather Summers, Capstone Publishing, 2004.

receptive to opportunities that come to you, listening to ideas and input from colleagues inside the company, as well as people outside the company – including weirdos! This is where crusty old big companies regularly slip up. Hoover could have acquired the rights to James Dyson's revolutionary vacuum cleaner quite easily and cheaply when he contacted them as an impoverished inventor with a great idea. Instead, they thought he was a nutter and dismissed the idea that great ideas could come from anyone other than themselves. As a result Dyson has now come to dominate the vacuum cleaner market, relegating Hoover to an also-ran. How different would the result have been if they had spared half an hour from their oh-so-busy diary to see him demonstrate his invention?

3. **Reacting quickly and expertly to opportunities.** Once an opportunity does reveal itself you need to act before it is snapped up by someone else or simply passes by. When Bill Gates and Paul Allen started Microsoft they believed that software was going to become the core of computing, and that hardware would be a low-margin business simply producing whatever was needed to run the software on (thereby ensuring their minds were open to opportunities in that area). They had been making sure that they were well networked in the emerging industry, and immediately spotted an opportunity when IBM decided not to write the operating system for its new computers in-house. They reacted quickly, and immediately accepted a contract to write it in the impossible timescale that IBM insisted on to ensure they won the contract. Then they used their well-established network again to find out that another programmer had developed software called QDOS (Quick and Dirty Operating System). They bought the rights, for just $50,000, and set about adapting this framework to become MS-DOS. The rest is history, but it all started with opening their minds to something specific, creating opportunities for finding what they wanted, and then reacting quickly and expertly. As a result, they've done okay for themselves.

4. **Persisting until the result is achieved.** I know many entrepreneurs, and have interviewed so many more, and one factor that is common to nearly all their stories is that there was (at least) one key point where normal people would have given up. The key to

success in all these cases was for the entrepreneur to pick themselves up and try again, and just keep going until it worked.

I'm going to assume now that you also believe in the entrepreneur's definition of luck, and move on to how they balance having a clear strategy with the ever-changing opportunities presented by luck.

A clear strategy is vital for the success of your business, and we'll look at that in more detail in Chapter 3 on Focus, but the difference between your entrepreneurial business and a stale big company is that you can react faster to changing markets and opportunities. You can make your own entrepreneurial luck, while the big company is firmly set on course for the strategy it planned two years ago, and the people close to the action who know about new opportunity aren't allowed to change the plans.

Of course, you can go too far the other way and confuse customers, shareholders, your team and even yourself by changing strategy unpredictably and frequently, just because you came up with a new idea, or read about a new trend in the paper, and you're convinced that this is your next piece of entrepreneurial luck.

So there clearly has to be a balance between long-term strategy and the seizing of opportunities as they arise. But how do successful entrepreneurs achieve this?

The key is to have a clear focus for your company that clearly and simply defines what you're about. This doesn't change, and gives you an easy first-stage measure to test new ideas against. We'll look at this in a lot more detail in the next chapter – Opportunity.

Confidence/paranoia

Entrepreneurs manage to achieve amazing things simply because they have the self-belief to go where others fear failure. They have such confidence in their own ability, the strength of their team, and their idea that it fires up their resilience (as we've already discussed) and they become unstoppable.

At the same time they are often paranoid. They're constantly looking over their shoulders at what competitors are doing, what technology is developing, where the fashion trends are going, what social and political changes are taking place and so on. They look for problems that might occur. They don't fall into the comfortable trap of assuming their competitors are stupid or second-rate. They respect them and expect them to make whatever moves are the smartest, and pose most danger to the entrepreneur. This helps them to be prepared for the worst that could happen, and therefore to be on top of any problems that do occur.

So at the same time as believing that they can do anything, they believe that there are myriad forces working against them and that they must work extra hard to justify their self-belief.

You can guess from these contradictory attitudes that an entrepreneur's brain is always busy! It can be difficult to balance all of these thoughts and beliefs. It will take time to find the right balance for you, so keep at it and don't be tempted to just go for one end of the scale or the other. If the balance isn't there you'll achieve far less.

2

The second secret: Opportunity

Opportunity is nectar for entrepreneur bees. A raw resource that doesn't appear to be much use to anybody else, but which entrepreneurs can find, gather and turn into honey.

Finding opportunities can be difficult enough. They are all around us, all the time, but there is so much going on in our lives and our world that we filter everything. These filters in our brain take in all the information from all our senses, keep only the stuff that we already know to be important, and chuck the rest away.

But some people become more alert and in control of this filtering process, and more aware of their environment. They take more active control of which information to discard and which to keep and process. They actively seek more stimuli and more information. Then, once they have this amazing resource in their brain, they create connections. They look for patterns, for chains of connections that create an opportunity.

These people are inventors or entrepreneurs. But don't confuse the two: inventors design 'things', entrepreneurs design businesses. You do not need to design a 'thing' in order to design a business.

Can you name one business that Richard Branson is in that involved him inventing the product from scratch? Opportunity does not equal invention.

Opportunity does not even equal a completely new idea for a business. You don't have to be first to market. Branson didn't launch the first record shop, the first record company or the first airline.

What Branson did in each case was to find an opportunity that, however small in difference from those spotted by other people, had enough of a divergence to attract his target customers. In Branson's case he always looks for opportunities in markets where the incumbent companies have become large, lazy and greedy. He enters the market with a fresh, value-for-money, caring offer to younger customers. He repeats the same pattern every time, just in a different line of business. Essentially he found the one type of opportunity, and then looked for it in many different industries.

Simply finding the opportunity to start a business does not equal success though; a lot of hard work is needed to capitalize on it. This requires the right attitude, talent and planning. Then, to maintain success, you constantly have to find new opportunities to provide your product or service to customers, and new opportunities to improve your business. We'll look at all that later in this chapter, but first let's explore how to find opportunity in the first place.

FINDING OR MAKING OPPORTUNITY

A lot of people make the mistake of thinking that opportunity is out of their control. It's just something that turns up if you're lucky (of course, they wouldn't think that if they'd read the chapter on attitude!).

Well, opportunity is entirely under your control. Opportunities are there to be found or, if you're a really good entrepreneur, you can make your own.

Opportunities from passion

What are your passions in leisure and in work? Chances are you're well placed to spot opportunities in this area if you open your eyes to them.

Entrepreneurs often start in or expand their businesses into areas in which they have a passion – perhaps even a hobby. Being passionate about something gives you extra focus on it, an extra interest in information regarding it, and an insight into how things work in that market.

You may also find that something from your hobby provides inspiration for an opportunity in another area.

Opportunities from skill

If you are skilled at something, then there is a tendency to simply turn this into your business opportunity. So a good gardener starts a gardening service, a good car mechanic starts a repair service, an IT whizz-kid starts a computer maintenance business, and someone who's good at drawing starts a graphic design company.

That's fine, and those businesses will do okay. But they will always rely on the founder, and the skills of the founder. Often they are doing little more than being a freelance worker.

The real opportunity in developing a skill into a business is in adding other elements to the mix, giving you a real difference compared to your competitors.

This can be a case of specializing – a mechanic who only repairs classic cars, or a designer who only designs book covers. Then you can really target a specific customer base who come to appreciate your speciality and will pay you more for your time than they would pay anyone else. This extra profit helps you to recruit and train other people in your business, allowing your company to grow beyond you and your skills alone.

It can also be a case of adding an extra level of service. There's a plumber in London who decided to start a plumbing company with a higher level of service for busy working people. They agree a specific time to show up, and they are punctual – you don't have to wait around all day for them. They train their staff to a very high level and they guarantee their work. The plumbers wear clean overalls and boots, and tidy up behind themselves, they don't leave a load of mess that you have to spend time clearing up.

Passion and skill are two key ways of adding to your abilities in order to create a better business, but you can combine any other opportunities in order to gain an advantage over the thousands of other electricians, builders, architects, accountants, gardeners, IT consultants, graphic designers, and so on.

Opportunities from contacts

The best entrepreneurs are people people. They're very different from the stereotype who only likes to talk about themselves, has a huge ego, and doesn't care about anyone else in any way.

Real entrepreneurs build and maintain good relationships with a wide variety of other people. They don't only value you because there's the potential for a quick sale to you in the short term, as people in professional services who have learnt about the importance of networking can. Entrepreneurs will value you based on your attitude and achievements above your status and net worth.

When real entrepreneurs have met people, they remember them. They remember their names, the conversation, and key facts. Now they're not all memory wizards; they might use notebooks, index cards, or computers in order to help them, but the point is that they value the contact and so make a point of remembering it in some way.

You might meet an entrepreneur at a party, and months later they could call you up to let you know that they've just met someone who would like to buy what you sell.

The key here is that they don't just keep a record of contacts, they actively make connections. So, when an opportunity presents itself they know all the key people they would need in order to take advantage of it.

How does your contacts book look? What connections could you make?

You can also make opportunities directly from the contacts that you have, but you need to know their problems and frustrations first. Get out to meet them, listen to them, keep your radar tuned for anything they mention that you can help them with, even if there's no direct reward in it for you.

Opportunities from trends

It's well worth keeping up to date with what's going on in the world. Normal people cocoon themselves in a reassuring world of sameness, reading the same newspaper every day, watching the same TV programmes.

To spot opportunities in trends, you need to be gathering as much information as you can. Read the *Financial Times* and a tabloid, read magazines like *FHM* and *Cosmopolitan* while also reading *Business Week* and *Business 2.0*. Listen to Radio 4 and Radio 5-Live as well as Radio 1 and commercial radio. Listen to people, watch people. Go shopping. Eat out. Gather information and note trends.

Some important current trends that could present opportunities are listed below.

1. People who are retired are now fitter, healthier and richer than ever before. They're not ready to get the pipe and slippers out – they want to live life to the full. They've had years of hard work, saving up their leisure time for when they retire, and now they're there. However, they find that the world is not ready for them yet. Products and services just aren't designed to their needs. What could you do to better serve this market?[2]

2. Standard family units aren't so standard anymore. People are living on their own much more, and there is a large rise in the number of young women living on their own. That means that individuals are having to take on the full range of purchasing decisions, shattering the stereotypes that women buy the white goods and furniture, while men buy the cars and lawnmowers. Everybody buys everything now. What opportunities does this present to make the product, service or even just the sales process more welcoming to non-stereotypical consumers?[3]

3. People have a heightened need for a sense of identity. This means they need to 'stand out from the crowd' and be individual. However, the catch is that they want to do this as part of a 'cool' group. So they want to be individual in a way that's the same as everyone else like them! This is why a certain group of people all want to download the latest ringtones to personalize their mobile phone, and there's a particular ringtone that is the latest 'must have'. Think of this trend as creating a series of tribes – what bonds

2 For more thoughts on this see *Re-Imagine*, Tom Peters, Dorling Kindersley, 2004.
3 For more on this see *Britain in 2010*, Professor Richard Scase, Capstone Publishing, 2000.

them is the identity that your product or service gives them. Look at the way that certain top of the range sports cars have a tribal following. The entertainment industry is the best at this, but any industry can do the same. You don't need to be targeting young, cool people to benefit from this effect: even Delia Smith and Marks & Spencer created tribal followings in their times. How can people form tribes around your product or service?

4. People are trading more with other individuals, using certain companies only as a 'hub' around which they can gather – look at eBay as the classic example. The great advantage to eBay is that they don't have to buy anything, make anything or ship anything – they just maintain the website that acts as the hub. Now an equivalent financial marketplace has launched, **www.zopa.com**, facilitating the lending of money between individuals. Cutting the big banks out of the transaction gives both parties better interest rates, and the company isn't risking its own money, just taking a fee on loans arranged in return for being the hub. How could you be a 'hub'?

5. Customers want to be more involved with the companies they buy from. They want to shape the products, tailoring them to their personalities or needs. They'll pay a premium in return.

6. People are focusing more and more of their spending on leisure items rather than essentials. This means two things: first, they're willing to spend to sort out the chores in their life to create more leisure time. This is great news for cleaners, gardeners, handymen, kitchen appliance makers, ready meals manufacturers and so on. Secondly, they're looking for fun things to spend their money on. This is great news for travel companies, computer companies, games companies, sports-related companies, car manufacturers and so on.

7. One trend in recent years has been the polarization of products and services to each end of the spectrum between 'really expensive but luxurious and full service' and 'really cheap but no service'. At the expensive end of the scale you have the growth of the private jet charter industry where you can be flown right to where you want to be, whenever it suits you, at short notice, with plenty of space and comfort. At the cheap end of the scale you have easyJet and

Ryanair where you usually have to book months in advance to get a good fare, you're herded around the airport like cattle from one queue to the next, you're crammed onto an aircraft and deposited at least half-an-hour's coach journey from even the outskirts of the city you want to go to. Meanwhile the middle ground in the air industry has been suffering from this polarization.

There is some reason to believe that the time is approaching for the consumers in some markets to want a return to the middle ground. They're getting fed up with spending so much of their time doing things like battling to assemble their own furniture just so they can save a few quid, or spending all their time on the phone to a support centre in India trying to communicate across continents what needs fixing about this thing they bought for £20 cheaper than the other thing that might have worked. Their time is too important to them now, and they're chasing fun and banishing hassle. Could you create an opportunity by providing a middle ground level of service for a middle ground price? You don't have to provide the whole thing, just the level of service on top of an existing product. There are people making a living by providing add-on services: they'll come to your house and assemble your IKEA furniture, set up and maintain your computer for you, or they'll list your items on eBay.

8. People want to make their mark on the world. They want to create blogs, podcasts and photo galleries (see **www.blogger.com**, **www.odeo.com** and **www.flickr.com** for examples of these). They want to write books and have them printed, paint pictures and have them on t-shirts, greeting cards or framed prints (see **www.lulu.com** and **www.cafepress.com** for examples). Services are cropping up to help people make music, compile family trees, write their autobiography, and much more. People are experimenting with their creativity more than ever before and they don't want to do it solely for their pleasure anymore, they want to tell the world. What can your business offer as a service to help them to do this?

Opportunities from problems

Entrepreneurial businesses, or new products for existing businesses, are frequently created when the founder, or someone they know, is faced with a problem in their life. It doesn't have to be a big problem, just an annoyance.

If you ever find yourself or anyone else saying, 'I wish they'd . . .', why don't you do it? Don't leave it to 'them', they'll never get round to it.

This is how James Dyson became a multimillionaire. He cleaned his house one day, and found that the vacuum cleaner had lost much of its suction because of the filter and bag system. He wished someone would design a better vacuum cleaner, but instead of leaving it at that he designed it himself.

There are many stories of women who started businesses providing products for new mothers as a result of their own frustrations. The world now has no-spill children's drinking cups, frozen organic baby food, and many other great products simply because mothers who had said, 'I wish someone would . . .' decided that they would be that someone.

Programme your brain to listen for every time you or someone you know comes across some problem or annoyance and says, 'I wish someone would . . .'.

If you are already running your company, then you can go a step further here. You need to know what frustrates your customers about the products or services you and your competitors provide. This can be a great opportunity to move leaps and bounds ahead.

Even Boeing, the aircraft manufacturer (by the way, why anyone would want to get in a flying tube made by a company whose name sounds like 'boing!' is beyond me) has got in on the act. They've launched an online group to seek passengers' ideas on how to make aircraft better in the future.

These companies are actively looking for the problems and frustrations of the customers, enabling them to get ahead of the competition by solving them. Every problem is an opportunity.

Opportunities from the unexpected

It has been said that the great breakthroughs in science are not marked by a researcher shouting, 'Eureka!' but mumbling, 'That's funny . . .' as they get an unexpected result from a test.

The same is so often true in business. You need to be on the lookout for the unexpected, something that breaks the accepted pattern.

Insider Knowledge

Ray Kroc was an entrepreneur who had risked his life savings and mortgaged his house to buy the exclusive rights to distribute an innovative milkshake mixer called The Multimixer. He had literally put everything he had into this opportunity, but that didn't stop him from spotting an unexpected result.

McDonald's hamburger stand in San Bernardino, California was operating eight Multimixers when its size and location suggested it should only need one or two. Ray was intrigued and drove hundreds of miles to visit the McDonald brothers' venture. When he arrived he was amazed at how many people were being served, and how quickly. The McDonald's idea was to serve a very limited menu, in a very standardized way, so that it could be done very quickly while maintaining the same quality for every burger, shake or portion of fries.

Ray Kroc saw the opportunity to take this very same format and roll it out to lots of other sites – all exactly the same, and all operating eight Multimixers! The McDonald brothers didn't see the same opportunity, so Ray bought the franchise rights then and there, and later he bought the whole business.

I think we can agree that it was worth Ray Kroc following up on that unexpected result. Some of you might even have been to one of his restaurants, as I understand he has a few nowadays.

Another great example of this is Wrigley's. Originally the Chicago-based company had nothing to do with chewing gum, they just came up with the idea of using it as a free giveaway with their products. But then they were brave enough to see the unexpected result that the chewing gum was more popular than anything else they did, and that became the entire focus of their business.

Opportunities to improve

You don't have to come up with completely new ideas in order to create opportunities. There are plenty of ways to create an opportunity by improving existing products or services for your target market.

In my view there are three ways to improve a product or service:

1. **Improve the location**. Bringing something from another area, or even another country, to where you live or taking something from where you live elsewhere in the world. Look at the growth of La Tasca Spanish tapas restaurants in the UK, and the spread of Harry Ramsden's fish and chips around the world. Both of these are the fruits of a pair of entrepreneurs, John Barnes and Richard Richardson.

   Sahar Hashemi started one of the first coffee bar chains in the UK (Coffee Republic) after seeing them in action in New York and missing them when she came home.

   Improving location is an often used way of creating opportunity in the food and drink industry, but it can also be applied to other areas. How could you use this to start a business, or to create new opportunities for your existing business? It's well worth travelling as much as you can to look for ideas abroad, and for opportunities to sell what you do in other countries.

2. **Improve the luxury**. A great way to create opportunities is to improve the luxury of an item in relation to your target consumer. This can mean making it more luxurious and more expensive – appealing to one target market, or less luxurious and cheaper – appealing to a completely different target market. As we discussed when we talked about trends, it can also mean heading for the middle ground in a marketplace that is currently polarized at either end.

3. **Improve the love**. This is a great way for smaller companies to create an opportunity in a marketplace of very big players. Consumers respond well to a bit of love. They can tell if a company really does love what it does, and the people it does it for, and they

reward this by being willing to pay higher prices and to repeat business.

There are very, very rare occasions when you can create an opportunity by removing the love – one example is the Indian restaurant that runs 'Balti Towers' nights, with a promise of poor service and rude staff that goes down a storm with customers who have a sense of humour. But the irony is that they're only pretending to remove the love, in reality they're doing this because they love what they do, and they love their customers – so this probably doesn't count as really removing the love.

Improving the love is a great way for entrepreneurs to carve a niche for themselves in amongst big businesses who can't compete with this. Look at the boom in small, fine food companies. They're more expensive than the supermarkets but customers will pay more for the best cheese in the world or their favourite real ale. A good question to ask yourself is, 'What can my business be the best in the world at?' and keep specializing until you have that niche. It's also hugely motivating for your staff to be seen as being part of the 'best in the world' at something.

So how can you create an opportunity by improving the location, luxury or love of a product or service that already exists? These ways of finding or making opportunity are just the start. There are many more. Opportunity is everywhere, you just need to open your eyes and ears to it. In fact, the most difficult challenge entrepreneurs have with opportunities is not finding them, but filtering them to find the right ones to pursue.[4]

OPPORTUNITY STAGES

Some people think that you only need to come up with an opportunity when you start your business, but that's not true. You need to be finding new opportunities constantly, whether this is in terms of new product

---

4 If you'd like more guidance on finding and analyzing opportunities I suggest *The New Business Road Test* (2nd ed), John Mullins, *Financial Times*/Prentice Hall, 2006.

lines, new markets, or new customers. After start-up, these are the key stages of finding new opportunities.

Opportunities for sales

Your business is nothing without sales. Whether you are selling to consumers or other businesses you need a strategy for creating sales opportunities.

The key sales opportunities, in increasing order of hard work, are:

1. **Selling more of your current product/service to existing customers.** These people already know who you are and what you do, and they've tried you out. If you were any good it should be easy to get them to buy from you again. If they don't buy from you again, alarm bells should be ringing in your head loudly enough to drive you mad. Find out why, and fix it quickly. Getting these customers to buy from you again is largely about staying in touch with them, so that they remember you and why they liked your service. We'll look at ways to do this in Chapter 6, Communication.

   But this is only half the story; on top of this communication you need to keep providing opportunities to buy. Don't make them do all the work. Either you need to create a reason for them to come into the shop, to open your catalogue, to visit your website or to ring you up and actually place an order – or you need to visit them or ring them up to give them that opportunity to buy.

   Selling more to existing customers also means increasing the amount that they spend with you each time they buy. Your salespeople need access to the information about a customer's previous order, or at least to the average order value of your business if you're in consumer sales, so that they can try to build on and beat that previous record. You can analyze the pattern of spending by your customers to create the real-world equivalent of Amazon's 'customers who bought X also bought A, B and C' initiative, or the equivalent of the treats at the checkout in the supermarket – anything that gets the customer to buy more this time than they did last time.

2. **Selling your current product/service more frequently to existing customers.** Chem-Dry is one of the most successful franchise stories in the UK (the UK head office that sells franchises in the UK is in turn franchised from the USA). It provides carpet cleaning services using its own patented range of products and machines, that it claims give a much better result than other methods. When I last met the founder of the UK business he told me that customers had their carpets cleaned once every three years, on average. His goal was to increase that to once every two years – and that alone was going to add millions of pounds in new sales. This was going to be achieved through an educational campaign, showing homeowners how much hidden dirt, insects and bacteria build up in a carpet over time, and what a difference it makes to clean your carpets once every two years, and by keeping track of which customers had their carpets cleaned when, then actively contacting them when the two-year anniversary approaches, instead of just waiting and hoping that they would remember.

   You can do the same. How frequently does each of your customers buy from you now? How could you increase that?

3. **Getting existing customers to bring new customers to you.** Referrals are a fantastic way to generate new business. If you've pleased your existing customers they will be happy to tell other people about you: they may be doing this already without you knowing. This can be even more powerful for you if you manage the process. Here are some ideas, with different ones being more or less suitable for different business types:

   a. Provide vouchers that give a discount or added value. Encourage customers to pass these on to friends.

   b. Organize a special event that customers can bring friends or colleagues along to, with your product or service as part of the event in some way.

   c. Offer customers rewards of some kind for introducing other people to your business.

   d. Make it clear to people that you would like them to recommend you to other people. Put a note on your letters, emails, invoices and so on that says something along the lines of, 'Did you like our work? Who else do you know that would like what we do? We'd be very grateful if you'd tell them about us'.

e. Offer to send a trial version of your product to three friends of each of your customers with a note from the customer who knows them.

4. **Creating new products/service for your customers.** Using all the ways of finding or creating opportunities that we talked about earlier in this chapter you can develop additional products or services that your existing and target customers would like to buy. Depending on your line of work you may need to do this just to stay in business, as some industries need constant innovation as a basic requirement. Where would Sony be if it were still trying to sell cassette Walkmans? Developing new things for your customers to buy is important to a large degree in any business.

5. **Finding new customers.** There's often a temptation to leave this until business starts drying up from existing customers, but you can't afford to. This is a very time-intensive and lengthy process, particularly in business-to-business sales, and your dry period will become a drought before you see any results. You need to develop a process to constantly feed new customers into your business, and we'll look at that in Chapter 5, Building.

You can get more advice on creating sales opportunities in your business in the book *Sold – How to make it easier for people to buy from you* by Steve Martin and Gary Colleran, published by Prentice Hall Business.

Opportunities to improve your business

Apart from increasing sales there is a constant need to improve the way your business is run.

1. **Do things better.** The best run companies are constantly learning how to improve what they do.

● When things go wrong they work out why (without apportioning blame) and work out how to prevent it happening again.

- They study other companies who are particularly successful at something and work out how they do this.

- They seek expert advice.

- They experiment.

- They seek customer opinion, experiences and advice.

- They bring in new, expert talent.

Every week they find ways to improve the quality and reliability of their products and services, putting them ever further ahead of the competition.

2. **Do things faster.** As companies grow, the successful ones increase their sales disproportionately to the increase in their costs. That means that they have to squeeze more time out of their talent and their resources by learning how to do everything faster; not just the manufacturing or service provision, but the administration work behind the scenes too. Look for every opportunity to do more things in less time.

   One way to do this is to standardize by finding anything that you do regularly and designing a uniform letter, form, contract, checklist or other document to streamline and standardize its execution in the future. We'll look at this in more detail in Chapter 5, Building.

3. **Do things more cheaply.** Sharp entrepreneurs are always looking to reduce costs. They search for new suppliers, haggle with existing ones, keep an ear to the ground to find out what other people are paying, and anything else they can do to find a cheaper way – but not at the expense of the things that are important to their company. When looking to cut out expense, take a look at your company focus (which we'll come to in Chapter 3, Focus) and attitudes, to check that you're not cutting back in areas that might harm your business by taking you away from the first or going against the second. Entrepreneurs only pursue cost reductions if it is not at the expense of the main essence of their company. For example, Innocent Drinks could make their drinks much more cheaply if they used concentrate instead of freshly squeezed fruit, but this would be against their focus and attitude, so they don't do it.

3

CHAPTER THREE
The third
secret: **Focus**

Once you have the right attitude and opportunity, you need to be focused. So many business owners spend their time being really busy and really stressed. They're always chasing their tails instead of achieving the success they originally hoped for.

Every time I talk to a highly successful entrepreneur about their business, I'm always struck by their focus. And every time I meet a small business owner whose business never quite worked, or that never quite got started properly, I'm always struck by their lack of focus: their minds dart from one thing to another without finishing anything, like butterflies that land on the most attractive flower for a few seconds before they flutter off to look for another.

Of course most of us are somewhere in between. We have the ability to focus when we want to, but we are also easily distracted by other things that look fun. I know that this is a failing of mine, and I'm constantly trying to work on it. In doing that I've had the luxury of studying friends with highly successful businesses and friends whose ventures failed. I've studied management literature, and the stories of hundreds of entrepreneurs. As a result I've developed the following simple system for finding what you should focus on as a business, focusing on it, and keeping focused.

COMPANY FOCUS

Your company exists for a reason, but what is that?

If you already run a business, try this exercise. Ask everyone in your company to write down on a piece of paper why the company exists, being completely honest – and therefore anonymous! You yourself should also do this. Then see if any two bits of paper say the same thing, and if any of the others match what you wrote down.

So many businesses lose track of why they operate, but most of the time that's because they don't even start out with a clear idea of why they exist!

The most successful companies are very, very clear about why they exist.

Find the focus

At the very start of your new business or a project to shape up your existing operation, you need to work out what it is that you should be focusing on as a company. To do this you need to know what your stakeholders want the business to achieve. A stakeholder is anyone who has an interdependent relationship with the company. We'll look at each group in turn – and remember that you are probably in more than one group.

Founder focus

Before you can focus on what you should be doing for your business, you need to spend some time thinking about what your business should be doing for you. It's a two-way deal: you work hard on building up a business, and in return it gives you some kind of reward.

First of all let's be clear that the reward you are looking for is not simply a job. You could easily get a job with another company, just like the one in your business, and have a much easier life. The job is something you put *in* to your business, not what you get *out*. So what *do* you want to get out?

When you contemplate this you're likely to start by thinking about how much money you want to earn. That's fine, but develop that thought further into what kind of lifestyle you're going to have because of that money. Build up pictures in your mind.

As a result of the work and investment you put into your business, what will your life feel like and look like in five years?

When you're busy running a company it's easy to lose track of your personal goals and just keep working and working to sustain the business. It's also very hard to take the time out to think about these dreams again.

However, I cannot stress enough how useful you will find it to do this. It is the first step of acquiring the focus you need to make your business so much more successful. You will gain renewed enthusiasm and energy. You will be more certain that you are going in the right direction.

Here are some simple ideas to help you picture what you are aiming for:

1. Get a big cork noticeboard to put on your wall. Go through magazines, websites, brochures, etc to find pictures of things that will be part of your life in ten years – the kind of house you will be living in, how the rooms will look, what car you'll drive, the kind of place you'll work in, where you'll go on holiday, what you'll do in your leisure time, and so on.

2. Stand back, take a serious look and think about whether this is really, really what you want, or whether it is just what you think you should want. A lot of people think they should want a huge house with a pool, a big Mercedes, and holidays in the Caribbean – when in their hearts they really want to live in a nice friendly community in a cosy house, or something other than the lifestyle of success that is portrayed in the media. It's important to be aiming for what you really want.

3. One of the Sunday papers has a piece called 'A day in the life of . . .' with a new person featured each week. Imagine that in five years they profile you. Write the article (about 500 words) about what your average day will be like.

This is just an overview because there are many other ideas on the subject of setting your long term personal goals elsewhere.

You really do need to get a clear idea of what it is you want. You should be able to sit in a quiet room and play it in your head like a movie. Do develop your picture of the future before you move onto the rest of this book, perhaps even go away somewhere for a day or two, specifically to spend time on it. You are shaping the rest of your life, so it is worth investing some thought in it!

Once you have a picture of your life in ten years, you will have an idea of what your company will need to reward you with during that period. This may start with being modest in the near term, but stepping up as time goes on. In deciding on the rewards you want, remember your different relationships with the business.

First, write down what you want from your company in your role as a shareholder. This could include the level of dividends, whether you wish to sell the company for a certain valuation in a particular timeframe, whether it needs to link in to other companies you own or will own, etc. It could also include what you want from the company to make you feel proud of owning it. A lot of shareholders only invest in ethical companies, fair trade companies, or companies that do other good works. What behaviour and attitude do you want the company to have to make you proud? These are the primary reasons your company exists, and should never be forgotten. You did not start this business to get a job, you started it to get your longer term rewards as a shareholder.

Next, write down what you want from your company in your role as a manager/employee. Work out what annual salary you want to be earning by when, how much time you want to spend at work, and what kind of work you want to be doing.

Finally, will there be a time when you move on from this company? How will that happen? What will you have earned when you leave? What opportunities will have been opened up to you by your success?

Investor focus

If you have any outside investors (people who have put money into the business but who are not founders or members of the team) then you need to consider what they expect the company to achieve too.

You may well already have a very clear idea of this, particularly if an investor is a venture capital firm, but if your investors are individuals then it might be more complex.

All investors will want the following, in differing amounts:

Financial reward. They're not giving money to charity. They are investing it in your business instead of putting it into the stock market, bonds, property or even just a savings account. They will want to see their sum earn them more money.

Pride. They will want to be proud of their association with you, not ashamed of it. That means being proud of the financial success, but also of the work that you do and the reputation that the business has.

Enjoyment. They're only human, and they'll want to get some level of enjoyment from being associated with you. This applies in particular to individual investors who may enjoy being in your industry, the products you make ('I liked it so much I bought the company'), or simply being part of the growth of a small business.

There might be other factors that come into play if your investors are friends or family.

The best way to find out what your investors are focused on achieving through investing in your business is to ask them.

Good questions are:

- Why did you want to invest in this business?

- When do you want to see a financial return, and what do you expect it to be?

- How long do you expect to own your shares for?

- When do you expect to earn a dividend, if at all? (They may be more interested in building the value of the business, ready for selling it.)

Summarize your findings into a one page 'Investor Focus'.

Talent focus

If you have an established company then you need to consider the wishes and ideas of its existing talent. There's more about 'the talent' in the next chapter, but essentially this is how we will view your staff. These are the people who will really make it happen in your business.

Your success rides on their talent.

If that statement makes you laugh, groan, roll your eyes or cry, then perhaps you need to encourage and help your team to change – altering their attitude, focus, talent, planning or communication, just as in the business as a whole. But, to put it gently, you may also want to change the employment status of some of the people in the team. You have to trust your gut instinct on this, and sometimes you may need to overrule your wish to be nice to everybody. It's much better that they go sooner rather than later, then they can find other work that is more suited to them. If they don't have the right attitude or talent they're going to really hate what's going to happen in the business over this period of improvement.

Once you have the right talent in your company, or at least a team that can become the talent during the process of building your business, you need to become very aware of what it is that they want to be rewarded with in return for their work. You must understand each individual's wants and desires, as everybody will be very different.

Some people look for security and a safe, long-term job. Some people want to work hard now to earn money to go off travelling or start a business. Some people want to see good opportunities to get promoted and get a better job title, better salary and better perks every couple of years. Some people want to feel they are doing valuable work and that this is recognized. Some people have a passion for the particular kind of work they do, or using a talent they have. Most people have combinations of these, in differing orders of priority.

In just the same way that you have worked out your long-term personal aspirations, you need to help each member of your team work out theirs. Then you and they need to establish how working for your company can help them achieve those aspirations. What do they really want as a reward for their work?

Also ask each member of your team – preferably informally and in person – the following questions:

- What does your company do? (Not a silly question! You'll probably get lots of different answers to this, which should highlight the need for a 'Company Focus'!)

- What makes them proud to work for your company now?

- How they would like the company to get better, i.e. what would give them more pride?

- Which parts of their work do they enjoy most?

- What do they think are the most important personal qualities for people in your company?

Summarize your findings into a one page 'Talent Focus' report.

Customer focus

You now know what it is that you want your company to reward you, your investors and your team with, but in order to be able to provide you with these things it has to earn money in return for providing products or services to customers.

So what does your company do for customers in order to earn that reward of money?

I'm sure you can list all the products and services you provide, but you may well decide to drop some of these and launch some new ones in the future. You need to decide on a higher vision of what your company does for its customers that is above the products and services, and is about the benefits you are providing for the customer, and what needs of theirs you are fulfilling.

To find out what your customers want from your business, you can simply create an opportunity to chat to them, and ask them:

- Why did you choose to buy from us in the first place?

- Why did you then choose to buy from us again?

- What do our products or services do for you? (What problems do they solve? How do they make your life/work easier? How do you use them?)

- Do you buy these things from anyone else as well?

- Are there any other companies who supply this kind of product or service that you have previously bought from but no longer use – and why did you stop using them?

- What different factors will influence your decision to buy less, or more, of these products/services from us in the future?

- What are the most important things you look for when selecting a supplier?

- What else could we do that would really help you?

It's best to ask these questions in conversation rather than by sending people questionnaires, as you'll be able to follow up on answers, and everyone is more guarded when they put things in writing. Another good tip is to be like a small child and ask 'Why?' a couple of times after they answer the main question. That'll really help you to get down to the important stuff, as their first answer will always be just touching the surface of the facts and their true feelings.

One added bonus is that just by you showing this kind of interest in them and their opinions they will be more inclined to buy from you. Now how's that for an incentive to go and ask these questions? This could be a good sales tool too.

Some people worry about asking their customers questions like these in case they simply reel off a list of complaints. But, if that does happen, it's far better that you do actually know about it so you can fix the problems before they take their business elsewhere. In reality though, if they're still your customers they're likely to be generally happy with what you do, so don't worry too much! They'll just be pleased you want to hear what they think.

Once you've done this research you'll have a good idea of what your customers want from your company, and hopefully a clear picture will emerge. If not, try dividing the results up into three groups by profitability – the top third of your customers, the middle third and the bottom third. This is often when a pattern emerges. You're obviously more interested in what the most profitable customers think!

If this still doesn't produce a pattern, further subdivide each group into two – customers it's a pleasure to do business with and customers who you wish you didn't have to work with. This may be because they are rude, aggressive, always trying it on, or anything else. You want to create a company that attracts more of the kind of customers that you enjoy doing business with, so it's better to listen to what that kind of customer wants more closely than the others.

Insider Knowledge

I know some entrepreneurs who won't take on any new customer that they wouldn't be happy to go for a night at the pub with, and they're much happier and less stressed because of it. This also has a side benefit – customers who are focused on price more than any other factor often turn out to be the ones who it's less enjoyable to deal with. They don't value having a good relationship with you, or the quality of your work – just the money. They will be rude and ruthless in order to get that best price.

Once you've identified what your best, most profitable customers want, you're one step closer to finding the focus for your company.[5]

Company focus

Now that you know what everyone wants from the company, you have the building blocks for working out what its focus should be.

A 'Company focus' is a statement that could include what you do, what you aspire to achieve, who you are as a workforce, and the attitudes you want to have. In essence it's the stuff that's so important to you as a group

---

5 This section 'Customer focus' is taken from *The Small Business Handbook*, pp. 2–4. I said just exactly what I wanted to say on the subject there, so it's reproduced here.

of people that you want it to be the focus of everything you do, every waking hour of every day.

You may well have worked for companies that had a 'mission statement' that was supposed to define this focus. It might have been something along the lines of, '*We strive to be the best sewage equipment company in the UK, empowering our employees to create world class innovative solutions and deliver high quality services to our customers, while earning year-on-year growth in profits for our shareholders.*'

I have two reactions to this kind of mission statement:

1. Yawn.

2. Pardon?

Apart from the lack of clarity and inspiration, I don't like the term mission statement anyway, because a mission is something that you need to finish. Putting a man on the moon by the end of the 1960's was a mission. Once that was done it was done, and the US space programme has been lost without a real driving focus since that time. You need to set a focus for your company that will always be true, no matter which projects come and go in the meantime.

But it does need to inspire people.

When I worked for the BBC, the Director General, John Birt, said the BBC's focus was to be 'the most efficient public service organization in the UK'.

'Yippee,' I used to think, 'I can't wait to get in to work this morning and be efficient relative to other public service organizations!'

The next Director General, Greg Dyke, changed this for the better, saying he wanted the BBC to be 'the most creative organization in the world'. Doesn't that feel more motivating and exciting?

At healthcare company Smith and Nephew their company focus is 'Helping people regain their lives'. Here you have a very worthy purpose, but note that it's not simply about saving lives, it's about a wider benefit that everyone in the company can work towards for their sphere of influence. As a result the company's human resources team is now making a big effort to help staff to achieve a better work/life balance – helping them to regain their lives.

In deciding on the focus for your company it can help to avoid being too specific about the actual products or services, as they can change over time, and to ensure that you're aiming for the benefits that come about as a result of your work.

Disney's focus is 'Making people happy'. That's very different to 'making fun cartoon films for the whole family'. Their goal also allows them to have theme parks, shops and lots of other sidelines, but all focused around the end result, the benefit, of making people happy.

To develop your company focus look through all the feedback you've received from customers and the talent. Are there any common themes? What are the perceived benefits of working with your company? What are the talent most proud of? What do they aspire to achieve?

It can be well worth spending some time planning a half-day away from the office for all the talent so that you can work on this focus together. You all have to want it, you all have to believe it, so why not all have some part in writing it? If you're going to do this be sure to plan the agenda carefully. Start by outlining what a company focus is, how you are going to spend the rest of the session, and how you will all decide what the focus is. Then perhaps ask certain individuals (with advance notice for preparation!) to do brief presentations on different aspects – a summary of feedback from customers, a summary of feedback from the talent, a summary of what your competitors are like, a summary of future trends in your marketplace, examples of the company focus of other organizations, etc. Then do an exercise listing benefits you bring to customers and talent as an organization before launching into a brainstorming session (possibly in different smaller groups). At this stage only write down all the ideas that come up, no matter how silly. Then bring all the ideas together and ask people to vote for three. You now have a shortlist. Finish the session there and give people some time to think about the shortlist before holding a final vote, or making your final decision, depending on your leadership style.

What is your company focus? Keep it really simple, but make sure that it will always be true, and that it is a worthy thing to aim for. You're going to spend a large part of your life working towards this focus – it had better be motivating!

Keep the focus

That's the hard work over, now the really hard work begins! It's so easy to have made the effort to identify your company focus, but to then forget about it and lose sight of it.

Your work as the leader of the company is mainly about keeping this focus, and we'll look now at some ideas and tools to help you with this.

Imaginary friends

Did you have an imaginary friend when you were a child? Well, now is the time when your skills of imagination are going to come in really useful. If you didn't you're going to need to practise this until the imaginary friends we develop for you are real enough in your head to have a conversation with. There is a reason behind this step on the road to madness. These imaginary friends are going to represent your typical target customers. Imagining them so closely is going to mean they can be present when you make key decisions in your company.

To begin the process, work with your core team to identify a few different types of target customers. A web design company might supply start-up businesses, established small companies and departments of larger businesses. They would create three imaginary friends, one for each type of customer.

For each friend build up a picture of exactly what they are like. Give them a name, background, likes/dislikes, hobbies, job title, and so on. How much do they know about your industry and products? What is their average working day like? What other things do they have to do apart from work with you? Where do they like to spend time? What other products do they buy? Where?

If you are targeting consumers rather than other businesspeople, you can think about where they shop, how they use your products, what their leisure activities are and so on.

Make sure that you get to know these imaginary friends really well – and that everyone in your company knows them too. Have them with you in meetings, when you visit your company's shops or other facilities, and at any time when you're making decisions about your business.

A simple trick like this will really help you keep focused on what your customers want.

Critical success factors

In order to deliver on your company focus, there will be a number of things that you absolutely must achieve. If you don't you'll either go out of business or fall short of your ambitions.

These are your critical success factors, and it's important to take the time to identify them.

This should be a part of your business planning process, but if you're not about to develop a business plan you can undertake the exercise on its own.

Let's begin by illustrating what I mean. The critical success factors for a commercial passenger flight between London and New York are:

1. The plane must be properly maintained, flightworthy and have sufficient fuel for the journey.

2. At least 150 tickets must be sold in order to break into profit on the flight – or there won't be many more flights.

3. The plane must get to New York.

There are lots of other things that need to be done: inflight catering, entertainment, baggage handling, etc, but they are all just important rather than critical.

Having these critical success factors will enable the managers at the airline to prioritize decisions they have to make – focusing on safety issues and sales in this instance.

If two problems came up, the fuel company hadn't quite put enough fuel on board for the safety margins required, and the onboard movie system had broken, the manager would easily be able to decide what to spend their time on.

The critical success factors for your business are likely to focus on similar things: sales, quality, safety, etc.

What absolutely must happen in your business for it to survive and achieve the plan? These are the critical success factors. Your maximum attention then needs to focus on these.

PERSONAL FOCUS

As an entrepreneur you have to achieve a huge amount in the same amount of time that everyone else has. You'll have the same length days, the same number of days in the week, and the same number of weeks in the year – yet you must get so much more done. That means you need to be very focused in what you do, how you do it and when you do it.

You've already identified the focus of the company, and therefore your job is to help the company move towards this. But you need to develop discipline and systems to help you do this without losing track of what's important.

Working at your best

The first step is to understand how you like to do the different kinds of work you need to do. When during the day do you enjoy doing sociable tasks like meetings, private chats, telephone calls, etc? When do you like doing administrative tasks? And finally, when do you need rest?

The rest of the world is channelled into nine to five days, but you don't have to be. Of course you still have to allow for when customers and other people you work with will be available, but that still leaves a lot of flexibility for you. I'm not good with mornings, so I don't tend to start work until ten, but I'm very good in the evenings so I like to work later. Some days of the week I'll take work home and do a session after dinner, often until 2am. A friend, who's also an entrepreneur, and I have often exchanged emails or phone calls in the late hours of night or early hours of the morning because we both like working then. I find those hours extremely productive. I can focus clearly on what needs to be done and plough through work that can take me hours in the daytime because of the interruptions – and my different mindset.

During the day I make phone calls that need to be made, and support my team members where necessary. In the evening I catch up with emails, work on proposals, and do other paperwork.

You can also use time that you wouldn't normally think of: baths, showers and the drive to work are great places to think over a particular issue in a creative way. Let your mind get into an almost dreamlike state and then just play movies in your head of what the solution to an issue might look like. I use these places to write speeches, prepare for important or difficult meetings (rehearsing all the possible challenges that might come up by picturing them in movie style in my head).

Entrepreneurs know that this dreamlike state can be incredibly useful. This is where flashes of inspiration come from. You don't have interruptions or other work you could be doing, just time to think and imagine. The more you try this, the more useful it will become as you exercise this part of your brain.

Getting organized

To use your time effectively you need to be well organized so that you do the right things at the right time, and for the minimum duration.

Before you can become organized you need to know what you are supposed to achieve. This information comes from two questions:

1. What is your personal focus?

2. What are your responsibilities?

These will tell you your priorities. Other stuff will need to be done, but not until you have done the things needed to achieve these priorities.

It's very, very easy to get sidetracked each day. The phone rings, people come over to ask you questions, and other tasks come up that seem more interesting.

The biggest challenge to making productive use of your time is the curse of the urgent. You know it's important to do the work to meet your priorities, but suddenly there's a crisis and you swing into action. You spend all your time fire-fighting instead of sticking to your focus and fulfilling your responsibilities.

In Chapter 5 on Building we'll look at some ways to construct systems to deal with these kind of problems, but a good start for now is to be very aware of what your focus and responsibilities are.

In developing my system for organizing myself I've been heavily influenced by efficiency guru David Allen and his 'Getting Things Done' framework.[6]

I've also noticed that other entrepreneurs use similar techniques in some of the areas, so the steps I outline below are a bit of a hybrid between my own system, ideas I've spotted entrepreneurs using at the coalface, and some of David's ideas – pulled together I believe this is an incredibly powerful system.

Notes system

Different people have different approaches to gathering notes and setting out their thoughts on paper.

Insider Knowledge

Richard Branson uses hardback notebooks in which he keeps endless lists, notes and scrawls. And 'scrawls' is the right word – he doesn't write neatly or even on the lines of the page much of the time. There are words scattered all over the page, some circled. There are doodles. It's a mess frankly, but it makes sense to him. He gathers his thoughts and notes in this way and then reviews them regularly to ensure that nothing gets forgotten. When he fills up one notebook he stores it safely in his office for reference and starts another. He now has an archive of his thoughts and meetings going back many years.

Other entrepreneurs use Mind Maps. This is a system of keeping notes that is particularly relevant to developing ideas and plans, but can also be used for notetaking in meetings. The idea was developed by Tony Buzan, an expert in the workings of the brain, to more closely resemble how our brains generate and store ideas than other systems of recall. Because this method is different to anything we've been taught at school it can take quite a bit of getting used to at first, but many people quickly become far more comfortable with it than any other method of notation.

Tool

How to do a Mind Map

1. Start with a blank, unlined sheet of paper.

2. Put the key idea in the centre and circle it.

3. Look for ideas related to the central idea and draw them, connected to the centre or each other by lines.

4. Get creative – draw little sketches, symbols, use colours – let your subconscious mind lead the way.

5. Work quickly. Don't worry about being neat or censoring your thoughts, just get it down on paper and edit later.

6. Look for further related ideas – and relationships between the ideas you have already put down.

7. There are no rules – whatever works for you is fine.

To find out more about Mind Mapping, read one of Tony Buzan's books.

Some people prefer to take notes electronically using a PDA or Tablet PC. Predictably, this is the method Bill Gates uses. The advantage of this is that your notes can be backed up, are searchable and can easily be emailed to others. The disadvantage is that it can put you off jotting down quick notes because you have to wait for the system to boot up, and batteries can run out, leaving you stranded.

---

6 Allen outlines this in more detail in *Getting Things Done*, Piatkus Books, 2002. I highly recommend it. You can also find out more at his website **www.davidco.com**.

I yearn for a good electronic notetaking method, and keep trying out anything new that comes along. I found the Tablet PC took so long to boot up and had such short battery life that it wasn't much use at all, and I found PDA's too fiddly to enter the information into. For the moment I'm stuck with the hardback notebook approach.

It doesn't matter how you take notes, all that matters is that:

1. You can quickly and easily jot down ideas that occur to you.

2. You are comfortable with the system, and find it easy to keep up.

3. You can carry it with you anywhere, because you never know when inspiration will strike.

4. You have somewhere to look for important information.

5. You can find notes when you look for them.

6. You can read and understand what you wrote!

So once you have a system, what do you need to keep a note of?

Ideas. Once you've got used to the entrepreneur's habit of creating and spotting opportunities, you'll need a way of recording them for future use.

Meeting notes. Remember that the most important things to write down are what decisions were reached, and what actions need to be taken, by whom, by when. You can also take notes during phone calls.

Useful or interesting information. This could be web addresses you want to visit, contact details for people, key points from newspaper articles, etc.

Action lists. Otherwise known as 'To-Do' lists, these are reminders to yourself about things you want to achieve.

Important discussions. Sometimes in meetings, on the phone, or even in casual discussions, someone will say something that could be important later. This could be an offer of something, an agreement to something you want, a promise of some kind, or anything else – but if it will have an important bearing on a business transaction then get down who said it, what they said (word for word), and when. Unfortunately not everyone is honourable in their business dealings and this kind of documentation can save you a lot of problems later. Richard Branson found notes like this extremely useful in a court case during his famous spat with British Airways – and I know many other entrepreneurs who have thanked their notetaking for getting them out of sticky situations and keeping other people honest, or regretted not having taken notes.

The key is to remember that your notebook is a gathering mechanism only, it won't wave a little flag at you to point out notes you need to be reminded of. Once you have collected the information you need to review it and feed it into your action system on a weekly basis. More on that shortly.

Reference system

With all the opportunities you will find and create, along with all the contacts you will make and all the research you will do on your market, customers, competitors, etc, you're going to have to store a lot of information.

What is more important is that you are going to want to be able to find it again! That means it needs to be organized – and not with a fancy, complicated system, just something nice and easy. Here are some ideas:

- **A filing cabinet drawer for each area of your responsibility.** For example, customers, staff, finance, etc.

- **A simple A–Z system.** This can take up as many filing cabinet drawers as you like, and everything goes into this one system. This is now my favoured filing system after having tried a couple of other combinations. I use square cut folders, clearly labelled and organized in one big A–Z system, so I look in the same system whether it's for a client's file, a project file, a supplier file or a research file. There's only ever one place to look. It sounds scary at first, but try it!

- **Digital system.** I would love to have a workable system for getting everything onto the computer so you could easily search for it, forward it to other people, etc – and it wouldn't take up lots of space in filing cabinets! Scanning is too labour-intensive to make this work at the moment though. If you can get a good, fast digital system working, do let me know!

Use whichever works best for you, but keep it as simple as possible. It's only a good system if you can always find stuff quickly.

Once you have a system, don't be afraid to use it, even for small items. If you often work late, keep a file labelled 'Takeaways' under 'T' and store all the local takeaway menus in there. Keep a file labelled 'Birthdays' with a store of blank cards in it, and ideas for presents that you might get people. The reference filing system can be useful well beyond the obvious core business supplier/customer/project role.

Diary system

When you're running a rapidly-growing business, life throws things at you far faster than you can deal with them. If you're not careful some of the important things you need to do will be forgotten in the rush to deal with the new stuff that has just appeared. That's why you need to ensure that you keep a useful diary. This can be a normal paper-based one, or an electronic one on your computer or PDA. This is one area where I find that electronics do win the day (hurray!), and I use Microsoft Outlook on my PC synchronized to my PDA.

You should record things in your diary as soon as you agree to them, and in the electronic version I find it highly useful to immediately write useful information in the notes section, such as directions, contact details of the person, the proposed agenda, etc.

I also find it useful to block out travel time as if it's an appointment itself – otherwise you don't leave early enough, or you book appointments too close together. You can also then allocate work to be done in the travel period, particularly if you are going by plane or train.

You can also record items in your diary of things that need to be done on a particular day, but not at a specific time – just put a note at the top of the page. This could be someone's birthday, a proposal you must do that day, but you can do it in-between your diary appointments, etc.

To be effective, your diary should tell you everything that absolutely has to be done today. You shouldn't be left wondering if there's anything else on a list somewhere else, or something in your intray. If it is important for today it's noted in your diary.

But even if you do use a hi-tech diary there are going to be bits of paper that relate to the tasks you have to do each day, and this is where a diary file can come in useful.

When I worked as a journalist at the BBC we relied on the 'diary file' to feed us reminders of stories to follow up, press releases that had been sent in advance, details of scheduled events we wanted to follow such as court hearings, etc, and details of special dates that might merit a feature such as a special anniversary of an event.

When I started in business I forgot about this method of planning, not thinking to transfer it from a newsroom to an office, but eventually I thought about it and haven't looked back. The diary file is fantastically useful.

Tool

A diary file

You need 43 square-cut folders and a filing cabinet drawer.

Create a folder for each month of the year, then create folders labelled '1' to '31'.

Arrange the folders so that tomorrow's date is at the front, with all the remaining dates in the month behind it. Then put next month's folder, with the 'used' date folders from this month behind that, ready for re-use. Then have the folders for the rest of the months of the year.

So if today is 5 September, you would have folders 6 to 31, then the October file, then folders 1 to 5, then folders November to September. (Because you've already emptied the 'September' file into the days of the week files by the start of the month, and it's now ready to receive diary items for the next year). Keep this cycle going each day.

The diary file means you can quickly pull out the information you need for each day, and you have a place where you know you can put things and be guaranteed to find them at the right time. In a business context that could include meeting agendas, directions, conference passes and travel tickets.

If I'm busy when something hits my desk, and I know it can wait, I'll pop it in the diary file for a week away to make sure it doesn't get lost or forgotten.

To make the diary file work you have to be disciplined. Have a routine that you will pull out the next day's diary file at the end of each day and have a quick check through it before leaving it on your desk or in your in-tray for use the next day. If you're going away, make sure you go through all the diary file folders for the dates you will be away – before you go.

Projects system

One rule that effective entrepreneurs seem to have is that everything is a project. That's a mindset that means they use simple project management skills to deal with things. Other people have a mass of 'things' to do, entrepreneurs have a series of current projects.

This doesn't mean they treat a project as a project management professional would, drawing big GANTT charts and huge lists of tasks with start dates, end dates and so on. They take a very informal approach to project management, but just dividing up the things that need to be done into clearly separate parcels of work really helps to keep track of things.

For example, if you need to recruit a new member of staff, a salesperson perhaps, this would become a project. It would get a folder in your reference system, but you also need a central place to keep track of your projects.

Different people like to do this in different ways, for example:

1. An index card for each project, held in a box on your desk.

2. Post-it notes on your noticeboard or the wall by your desk.

3. Just a simple page of A4 with a list of projects, or any other way you want to keep a list that you can update. This is the method I use.

It only needs to be a list of the project names, nothing else. Why? Because its only purpose is to remind you of what projects you have to enable you to find the files, and to prompt you to consider what needs to be done next in each.

The most common reason for projects stalling is people forgetting they exist, or neglecting to put the next step on the list of work to be done. Which leads us to the 'action' system.

Action system

Entrepreneurs are about action – focused action. But this doesn't happen by chance. It's enabled by a system of action planning which can be conscious or subconscious, and that in turn is enabled by an action mindset.

Other businesspeople skip the step of creating projects in order to trigger the required next actions, and simply put the entire thing on their to-do list. How many people would just put 'recruit new salesperson' on their to-do list? That's such a big, involved, unspecific thing that you will always keep putting it off. It's not an action, it's an outcome.

An action-oriented entrepreneur would have that on their project list, and would then identify the next action step that needs to be taken – 'design Talent Cake for new sales role'. This would go on their action list. (We'll discuss Talent Cakes in the next chapter.)

Once that action has been completed that would trigger them to consider what the next step is and put that on their action list – 'write copy for job advert'. On completing that they would decide the next action and put that on their list too – 'brief designer to create job advert' – and they may decide to add other actions simultaneously – 'brief web designer to add job on recruitment page of website', and 'email all staff to ask them to put the details of the job out to their networks'.

Completing any action triggers the question, 'What's next?' Finishing an agenda item in a meeting triggers the question, 'What's the next action?' Finishing a telephone call triggers the question, 'What's the next action?' Then you put it on your action list.

But things can still fall through the gaps, we're only human, so that means you need to refer to your projects list regularly (I suggest weekly) and check that there is a next action in your system. If not, add one.

At the end of each day you should review the day's events and update your action list with anything you have agreed to do, and anything else that is in your mind.

Action lists are things that you will do around the stuff written in your diary, so if an action has to be done at a specific time or on a specific day, add it to your diary.

Delegation system

To enable effective delegation you need a system.

The first thing to bear in mind is that, except to your PA, it's best to delegate projects rather than specific actions. That means you need to keep track of them in a similar way to your own projects: start a list called 'Delegated Projects' that you treat in just the same way. Record each project you delegate, who you delegate it to, and when you delegated it. If necessary you can also have a file in your reference system to keep notes and supporting material.

Once a week review your Delegated Projects list and decide whether you need to take any action on them. This could be, 'ask Emma for progress update on recruitment of sales manager'. You may decide that no next action is required of you, if your team have been keeping you properly up to date and there are no issues with the project.

It's simple but it works.

We'll come back to delegation again in Chapter 4, Talent.

Review system

Now that you have systems for notes, reference, diary, projects, action and delegation, you need a system to keep all these plates spinning. This is called the review system.

It's well worth having a brief review at the end of each day to catch yourself with everything fresh in your mind:

1. Check your day's notes. Add things to your reference system, diary, projects list, action list or delegation list.

2. Tick things off your action list that you've completed.

3. Check the diary file for the next day.

4. Add anything to your diary or action list as necessary.

5. Check through your diary for the next day and ensure everything you need is on your desk or in your briefcase.

6. Go home with a clear head!

Your main review is best held around the end of the week. Some people like to do this on Friday at lunchtime in case they find anything they absolutely must do before everyone goes home at the end of the week; others prefer to do it after everyone's gone home (some people do it at the weekend), so that they have peace and quiet. Others prefer to do it at the start of the week. I like to do it right at the end of Friday, once everyone has gone home, to allow me to clear my head. Here's the checklist for the weekly review:

1. Do the daily review.

2. Check your projects list. Does every project have a next action?

3. Check your delegated projects list. Do you need to add an action to any of them?

4. Do you need to create any reference files for things on your desk, in your in-tray, etc? Get it done.

5. Update your diary filing system by checking through the next month's folder and moving stuff into the day folders that have passed and gone into the next month.

6. Check through your diary for the week ahead.

7. Offload anything else that is in your head to the reference system, diary, or action list.

8. Go home with a clear head!

A system like this takes a bit of time and effort before it becomes second nature, but once you can adopt this as your normal way of working you'll be amazed how much more you can get done, and how many more things you can keep track of. That's what it takes to be a real entrepreneur instead of just being a small business owner.

THINKING AND ACTING

This is a challenge of being the leader of the business. You have to spend time thinking about your business as part of your responsibility to 'build' it (see Chapter 5, Building). But you can't sit around all day thinking, you need to be doing something.

Your focus will help you to decide what needs doing when you do spring into action, but how do you get the right balance between thinking and action?

It can be easy to let the thinking time get swamped by the doing time, so I find it useful to create thinking periods. Perhaps stay in the office for a while once everyone's gone. It can help, if something pops into your brain that you need to reflect on, to add it to your action system (ironically) and then check for 'think about' action items during your set aside blocks for contemplation.

But some people can get too wrapped up in reflection and just end up procrastinating, delaying decisions so that they never actually get to the action part.

Entrepreneurs have a system of 'Ready-Fire-Aim-Fire Again'. That is, that they try stuff quickly, check the result, use this information to improve, and then try again. They risk having a few misses in order to have swift action.

If an idea occurs to them and their gut instinct is that it's good and it fits the focus, then they will very quickly give it a go – even in just a basic way.

Insider Knowledge

The guys at Innocent Drinks had this idea for making fruit smoothies, and they could have sat around forever thinking about their plans. Instead they very quickly organized to go to a local music festival with their drinks to try selling them. They had a sign above two bins that said, 'Should we give up our day jobs to make these drinks full time?' and one bin was marked 'Yes', the other was marked 'No'. They asked customers to put their finished cup in one of the bins to vote – and you can guess the result.

The key here is that they didn't hang around. Their gut instinct said the idea was right and they very quickly went out to try it. They didn't wait until they could afford to buy a nice display stand, or a van – they just did it with a table, a mixer, lots of fruit and some bins. It was an amateur set-up but it worked to test the idea.

Take time to think about the big issues in your business, but don't be scared of acting. Realize when the time has come to act, even in a small, experimental way, and just do it.

FOCUSING YOUR TEAM

It's in your interests to help your team remain focused. You can start by helping them develop a system like the one outlined for you in this chapter, but it's best to wait until you have become proficient in it, and can demonstrate its advantages, otherwise people will be a little cynical about it.

We'll look in detail at leading and focusing your team in the next chapter.

CHAPTER FOUR
The fourth secret: Talent

Nothing will get done in your business without the right people. That may just be you, or you may need hundreds of staff – but you still need an effective way of harnessing that talent and putting it to work in your business.

Talent management in small business can be erratic at best. Small business owners are either scared of becoming the boss or they become a mini-dictator.

The best entrepreneurs have a skill for finding the right people and then motivating and managing them to achieve amazing things. This skill can be instinctive, but it can also be learned and practised.

I've found it best to develop a system to do this – not a big company-style, complicated system – just a simple but effective one for use in fast-growth companies.

THE TALENT SYSTEM

This system is designed for entrepreneurial companies. It's simple, so it can be used by start-ups, but it's effective enough to grow with you. Like everything it's been developed from my own experience, and also from seeing how lots of entrepreneurs managed this issue without a formal system, but by using parts of this technique informally. It's much more powerful to bring it all together.

The principles of the Talent System

The Talent System is based on the key principle that there are three elements to the expectations you have of your staff:

- Attitude.

- Skills.

- Responsibilities.

Attitude is more important than anything else. It's whether people are honest, enthusiastic, friendly, keen to learn and so on.

Skills are what they need to know, and be good at, in order to do their job. For example: networking, writing letters, programming computers, operating machines, driving a vehicle, etc.

Responsibilities are what you expect them to do, and to what level. For example, it could be a salesperson's responsibility to sign up three new customers a month. Your team can only carry out these responsibilities properly if they have the right attitude and skills.

The most important thing to remember is that it all starts with attitude! Your life will be so much easier if you recruit people based on their attitude and then train them in the skills necessary to take on the responsibilities, than if you take on staff with the right skills and try to get them to have the right attitude.

It's amazing how quickly people with the right mindset can pick up the skills you require, but people's attitudes are generally very difficult to change.

You'll notice in this book how attitude is the most important thing for you to master about being an entrepreneur – I even put it right at the front! Well, it's the same for every other job in an entrepreneurial company.

Your team in the future

When you're in the early stages of a business it can be hard to imagine that there'll ever be anyone but you doing all the things that need to be done. If you already have a business with staff it can be easy to lose track of the future growth amid the challenges presented each day.

It's also easy to fall into the trap of never actually designing what your company will look like in the future, and just adding a new person here or there as stresses build up in particular areas, growing haphazardly.

It can really help to take a bit of time to work out what structure your company is likely to have, and then work back from there to how it should be now – designing your business in reverse.

Start by itemizing all the responsibilities that will need to be taken care of in your fully grown company. The basic beginnings of a typical responsibilities list might look like this:

- Manage existing customer accounts.

- Identify and research new customers.

- Approach new customers.

- Win business from new customers.

- Communicate with the trade press.

- Communicate with the local press.

- Communicate with shareholders.

- Do email newsletters.

- Update the website.

- Manage external suppliers.

- Recruit new talent.

- Train talent.

- Administrate regarding talent (contracts, holidays, sick leave, other administration tasks, etc).

- Invoice customers.

- Chase payments from customers.

- Pay suppliers.

- Plan the finances.

- Manage the finances.

- Prepare monthly management accounts.

- Make certain parts of products.

- Test products for quality.

- Provide certain services.

And so on, and so on.

It's certainly not the case that each responsibility represents a person's job, just that it needs doing by somebody. Each person in your company will be responsible for many tasks.

It can help to put each of these tasks on a sticky-note so that you can move them around, and then put all the jobs into groups representing the teams you'll have in your company – sales, marketing, finance, production, support, etc. The teams you decide to create, and what you choose to call them, are up to you.

It's not essential now, but if you want to get a more detailed picture of what your company will be like, you can divide the sticky-notes from each team up further, so that each little group is a person and their responsibilities. You may need to make copies of some notes so that more than one person can be doing the same things if some of the tasks require that.

Now you have a rough and ready organization chart for the future of your company, with all the tasks broken down to either team or individual level. Copy it onto a big sheet of paper to keep and refer to.

Your present team

The next step of the Talent System is to repeat the exercise above, but to create the organization to fit your circumstances now.

Start with the same set of sticky-notes that you laid out for your future organization chart and go through each team, removing the tasks that don't need to be done yet in your business. Once you're finished you'll be left with just what needs managing now.

You may be surprised to see how few notes you remove! In part that will be because you don't know what many of the future tasks will be, but it will also be because at this stage of your business the same things need doing, just for fewer customers. Also, in the future, you will have more finance/administration/support talent to take on a lot of work that will fall to you and your current team.

Next, group the tasks you've identified in the teams on your current organization chart into jobs.

You may find that there are a different number of jobs to those actually present in the company. You may find that the division of tasks is different in theory compared to reality. If so, think about the difference and decide if this suggests that you need to make changes.

The Talent Cake

Okay, we've covered a lot so far, and I hope you've found it useful and thought-provoking, with some ideas you can put into action already, but we're about to work through what I think is the most useful tool in the whole book.

I've worked in big companies and I hated the way they did job descriptions, appraisals, training plans, etc. It was all pages and pages of waffle to show that they'd done it. As soon as the appraisal was over it could be filed away and forgotten about. It was simply a box-ticking exercise because no one could see the value of it.

But I've also run my own businesses, and know that my initial approach of simply ignoring the whole idea of clearly defining a job, and assessing how well someone is doing at that job, doesn't work for most people. Some people learned to love it – the freedom to make the job their own – but others were either daunted by the undefined and unmeasured nature of their role, or they didn't realize that this freedom comes with responsibility. People are so used to being told what to do, how to do it, and when to do it at school and in working life, that they don't always know how to react if those demands aren't there.

It's much better to have some kind of simple system to outline what everybody expects. But how? I've been looking for an idea that achieves this for some years. How do you strike the balance between simplicity and effectiveness, and avoid creating boring, complicated paperwork? I wanted a simple idea that worked. I searched everywhere without luck.

Then, about two years ago, one of my mentors (Steve McDermott, a top motivational speaker) sowed a seed in my mind that was developed further by working with management guru Tom Peters. I've worked on developing this into a viable idea for some time, and the Talent Cake is the result.

Picture the Talent Cake

The Talent Cake looks like a wedding cake (after all, working in a fast-growing entrepreneurial company is not far off a marriage in terms of commitment and time!), three layers stacked one above the other, getting slightly smaller as they go up. It's drawn on one side of a sheet of paper, and it's everything you need to define someone's job and assess them. Each cake is divided into slices, with each slice representing one part of that layer.

Company Name ....
Company Focus ....
Your Name ....

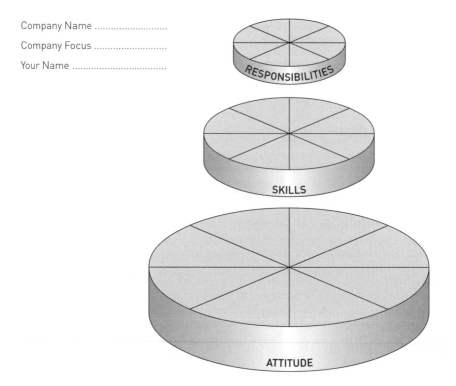

The principles of the Talent Cake

As stated earlier, the expectations you have of each of the members of your team are based around three factors:

1. Their Attitude.

2. Their Skills.

3. Their Responsibilities.

Attitude is the bottom cake, the base on which everything else is built. If their attitude is poor, it's unlikely you'll be happy with the rest of their work. Attitudes you're likely to want in your team are:

- Honesty.

- Enthusiasm.

- Helpfulness.

- Keenness to learn, and so on.

So you'd divide this layer into slices with one for each of the attitudes you identify. You can have as few as you like, but don't have too many as people will never remember them all. You may choose attitudes that fit with your company attitude, and others that are specific to their role. Don't be scared to use adjectives to roughly describe the level of attitude you expect, such as 'Jaw-droppingly inventive' for a product designer.

Skills is the next layer up on the cake, and is the range of abilities that you expect them to display in their work. Skills can be learned, so as someone develops their career with you, they can also grow their skills. Sample slices here might be: 'Using Microsoft Office software', 'Creating and maintaining a network of contacts', 'Selling over the phone', 'Managing projects', 'Developing new product ideas', etc.

Responsibilities are on the top cake, which rests on top of Attitude and Skills, because being able to meet their responsibilities depends entirely on the other two. Responsibilities are particular tasks, targets or other expectations of work that the person will do in their job. This layer might include: 'Produce monthly management accounts by the 14th of each month', 'Generate 20 new leads a month', 'Secure three new customers a month', 'Increase average sale value to £200 by July', and so on, depending on what the job is.

Baking a Talent Cake

At the top of every Talent Cake goes the company focus. The job only exists to support that focus, so it's important to make it clear. See Chapter 3 on Focus for a recap.

Below the Company Focus, the rest of the Talent Cake relates to the specific role.

Let's take the example of a Customer Service Assistant in a reasonably small company. We do this by working backwards, top to bottom:

We start by defining the Responsibilities layer. Our slices will be:

1. Helping customers who contact us by phone, email or letter.

2. Solving customers' problems quickly and to their satisfaction.

3. Helping to improve what we do to avoid future problems.

4. Keeping the sales team informed of contact from their customers.

5. Spotting opportunities to help customers through new sales/upgrades.

Then we look at the Skills that will be needed to underpin these responsibilities. Our slices on this layer will be:

1. Good computer skills.

2. Great phone manner.

3. Clear, professional letter writing.

4. Excellent communication skills.

5. Sales skills.

Finally we look at the Attitudes that are needed as a base on which to build the Skills and Responsibilities. The slices on this layer could be:

1. Amazingly helpful.

2. Very friendly.

3. Imaginative.

4. Attentive to detail.

I think that's easy and clear enough, don't you? Now this one sheet of paper can be used to:

- Help write a job advert.

- Interview the candidates.

- Brief them on their first day.

- Review their progress after a few weeks or months.

- Form the basis for a monthly review or mentoring meeting.

- Form the basis for the annual appraisal.

- Help identify training requirements.

- Help plan career progression – which slices do they leave behind, and which do they add?

Company Name ....

Company Focus ....

Your Name ....

RESPONSIBILITIES

SKILLS

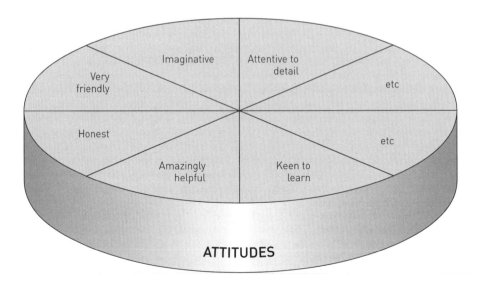

ATTITUDES

Recruiting talent using the Talent Cake

When you decide that the growing responsibilities in the business mean a new member of the team is needed, first ask if that person needs to be recruited on to staff or if the role can be handled by an outside supplier or a freelancer.

If it's a back-office role with little customer contact, or a specialist role that is outside your company focus, then it may be best to use someone outside the business. But if the role will involve customer contact and is important with regard to focus, it is best to bring someone into your team.

If you do decide to recruit a new member of staff, draw up the Talent Cake for the position.

You will now have a picture of the Attitude and Skills you are looking for. Where are you likely to find someone like that? Where will they hang out?

The challenge for entrepreneurial companies is often that the kind of people they actually want aren't really in the employment market browsing ads, they're busy doing their jobs. That means you need to be creative in how you reach them. Put advertisements on your website, on your products, or on big signs wherever you have premises. Get all your staff to put the message out to their networks or put it in the footer of all your emails.

Entrepreneurial businesses are normally looking for people within a certain geographic area (as they can't normally offer relocation packages) so that helps to narrow the search. Perhaps you think the individuals you want will buy their lunch in particular cafés or restaurants. Can you put notices there?

Remember that you are primarily looking for someone with the right attitude – which means your advertisement should have the right attitude too. Don't make it a stuffy, formal ad if you want someone bright, bubbly and creative. Think about what would attract people with the mindset you want.

When it comes to selecting people for interview, remember that it's all about attitude (have I mentioned that yet?). If you are looking for someone with a good attention to detail, have they shown this in their application? Are things spelt properly? Is it neat?

If you're looking for someone creative, have they shown this attitude well, or have they just done a bog-standard CV like everyone else? The contents of a CV matter far less than the attitudes that are demonstrated by the way the CV is presented.

But an application can also be about more than the CV. Perhaps you want to ask salespeople to give you a call?

At interview time, remember to ask questions whose answers will help you assess attitudes, and be sure to be on the lookout for any clues as to these. Too often people are looking for skills or experience at interview, and not paying enough attention to points of view and approaches to life.

Assessing using the Talent Cake

It's up to you how you use the Talent Cake to assess people. Some entrepreneurs like to have a regular six-monthly review with their team, others prefer it to be informal and occasional. Choose what suits your business, and your team, best.

In any review, remember to focus mainly on the attitudes! Then when you're sure they are all present and correct, you can move on to skills and responsibilities.

Insider Knowledge

One entrepreneur told me that he is very, very tough on people who don't show the right approach. He assesses people on attitude and performance. If they show the right attitude and the right performance, then of course they stay and do well. If the staff member demonstrates neither the correct attitude nor performance, then of course they go!

▶

The interesting thing is what happens to the remaining people. Those who show the right attitude but poor performance are kept on – but given more training and support or moved into another role. Those who show the right performance but repeatedly fail to get the right attitude are out on their ear – even if they are the company's star salesperson. That's a tough decision to make, but his company is very successful as a result – and a happy place to work.

You can take similar action. People who don't show the right attitudes should be treated very sternly – think of Gordon Ramsay. Those who have the right attitude but not the right skills, and are failing to meet their responsibilities, should be trained or moved.

Entrepreneurial businesses often find that they have recruited somebody to do a particular job, and that person is a wonderful fit for the company in attitude, but they're just not performing well in the position. Given the opportunity to change jobs within the same company, that person frequently shines. Allowing people to switch jobs, even to completely unrelated roles, can often bring out talents in them that even they didn't know they had. Give people with the right attitude every opportunity to prove themselves.

YOUR OWN TALENT

I was very impressed to find out that entrepreneurs place such high value on continuously developing their own talents. They don't reach some pinnacle of success and decide, 'Right, that's it. I know it all.' They're almost addicted to learning new stuff. It comes back to the attitude of being open, and the obsession with finding opportunities.

They know that the more they learn and the better they become, the more opportunities will present themselves – and the better they will be able to take advantage of them.

Becoming self-aware

Take a few moments to give yourself an honest appraisal. What are your big talents? What stuff are you quite good at? And what aren't you very good at?

Be honest with yourself.

Where do you need/want to be?

Now, write a list of the attitudes and skills you will need to have in order to achieve everything that you want to achieve.

What new things do you need to learn? In what areas do you need to improve?

Do you need to learn people skills? Sales skills? Finance stuff? Industry knowledge? IT skills? There are hundreds of areas in which entrepreneurs can benefit by improving their skills – what are the key ones for you?

Make a list of your priorities for learning in the next six months.

How will you develop?

You now know what you would like to learn, but how will you go about gaining this new knowledge? Here are some ideas:

- Get a friend or colleague to mentor you.
- Read books.
- Listen to audio-books.
- Take an online e-learning course.
- Research the subject on the web.
- Go on a training course.
- Try out some new ideas in practice.

Different people learn in different ways, so feel free to plan your own training in any way you like. Some people hate classroom training and prefer to teach themselves from books and the web (that's my preferred way!).

The trick is to plan the training into your diary – and do it! Otherwise it's always so easily left until 'another day' which never comes.

YOUR TEAM

In the Building chapter we'll look at the actual dynamics of your team, and how to create such a group. In this section we'll look at the talents you'll need in order to head up the team. Remember as well that your attitudes (covered earlier) are vital to your role.

Leadership

This is one of the most difficult skills for a first-time entrepreneur to learn, if it doesn't come naturally. Your team will be looking to you for direction and motivation. You will be their leader.

That means they will look to you for an example of how they should behave and how hard they should work.

Being a leader is *not* about being everybody's best friend. It's about being respected, and rallying people around the company focus. If people feel the focus is valuable, and they respect you, then you and your team can achieve great things.

Don't put your energy into trying to make people like you. That will often have the opposite effect. People like strong leaders that they can admire.

Again, an example of a good leader is TV chef Gordon Ramsay. Watch his programmes to see him in action. He doesn't stand around the cooker getting chummy with trainee chefs about their weekends. He demands respect, expects perfection, and is prepared to lead by example. If he finds a dirty kitchen he gets down on his hands and knees with a scrubbing brush along with everyone else.

For another example, watch Martin Sheen play President Bartlett in 'The West Wing' TV series. He doesn't try to be best friends with his team. He holds them to high standards and demands respect. His focus is on what he believes it is right for them to do in their work.

With both of these examples, people who believe in the focus of the organization and who work hard like their leader as well as respecting them. People who don't care about the focus and don't work hard fall out with them.

Who else do you think of as a great leader? What did they do? Have you encountered any bad leaders? What were they doing wrong?

So few people that take on a leadership position spend any time thinking about what it is that makes great leaders. You, along with the great entrepreneurs, can be the exception. Read books about great leaders, watch films about them – that is some of the best leadership training you can have!

Your work as a leader is to:

1. Set the company focus, and keep everyone focused on it.

2. Set the standards for attitude and style of work – mainly by example.

3. Give recognition to those who meet or exceed these standards – promptly and fairly.

4. Discipline those who do not meet these standards – promptly and firmly, but fairly.

That's the main part of the work. If you get this right, everything else will be much easier, because you will have a loyal and hard-working team to support you.

In the early years of my business I wasn't at all sure about becoming a 'boss'. I'd had some bad bosses, and thought that the way all the staff felt about them was the way all staff felt about all bosses.

It took me a few years, and seeing how other entrepreneurs worked, before I began to become comfortable with being a leader. I'm still very much a learner – but I'm now much more comfortable with being in charge.

It is your responsibility to become the leader of your organization. People need, and want, leadership. You are in charge – it's your job.

Delegation

As the leader of the organization it is not your job to do everything. Some people who start a business have problems with this. Even when they grow and have to take on staff they end up still fiddling around with the kind of work they used to do, rather than giving themselves the necessary promotion to manage the staff and lead the business.

Even those who realize that they need to start delegating can end up doing it badly. They either meddle, giving specific instructions on how to do every little bit of the job and constantly checking up on the staff member, or they give away the job and then seemingly forget about it, making the employee feel it was unimportant or that the boss didn't appreciate their work.

Effective delegation takes quite a bit of practice and effort to get right, but the reward is a much slicker, more efficient and happier organization.

The first hurdle to get over is that the people you employ *expect* you to give them jobs to do. Don't feel bad at suddenly being the boss and telling people what needs to be done. Not everyone wants to be an entrepreneur and be in charge. Most people want to be led.

5

CHAPTER FIVE

The fifth secret: Building

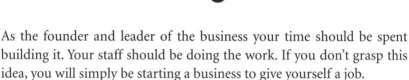

As the founder and leader of the business your time should be spent building it. Your staff should be doing the work. If you don't grasp this idea, you will simply be starting a business to give yourself a job.

In this chapter we'll look at how to shake off the shackles of small business ownership and discover the freedom of being a true entrepreneur – building for the future.

BUILDING A LASTING BUSINESS

Will your business still be around in ten years? Fifty? A hundred?

If not, when do you plan to close it, and how? Why would you close it? Do you just not dare to think that you might create something that long-lasting?

If it will be around for that long, will you be? My guess is that not many of you will still be running your business in a hundred years – and many of you might prefer not to be heavily involved in your business in fifty, twenty or even ten years.

The entrepreneurial ideal is to create something that lives on without you, to create lasting wealth for you and your family, and/or to leave a legacy to the world.

Jim Collins and Jerry Porras in their book *Built to Last* (which has been a must-read for corporate executives since its publication, but I highly recommend it for entrepreneurs too) talk about the leader of a business 'building a clock rather than telling the time'. You want a business that can stand on its own and run without you being there all day, every day. That is where you create the most value for a future potential sale, or create a better lifestyle for yourself in the future. It also gives your team the best security – the business will still run if you and a bus have a material disagreement.

If you want to achieve this you have to make the business able to work without you.

Stop for a moment, and picture yourself going away for a three-month holiday, without any contact with your company at all. Not one email, not one phone call. How do you feel about that? What state would the business be in when you got back?

If it worries you and you think that it might cause problems, then you've got some work to do. You need to create teams and systems that run smoothly without you there to micro-manage.

First you need to create a clear understanding of the company's focus and attitude. This is often known as the 'brand' – although people wrongly tend to think a brand is just about a nifty logo. It's actually the compass that will help everyone in your business to know what the 'right thing' to do is, at any time. If they have this compass to guide them, they won't need you to shout 'turn left' or any other specific instruction as to what to do, they will be able to navigate their own way.

Next you need to focus a huge amount of time and energy in developing the right pool of talent in the company. Building the team, then encouraging the right attitudes, developing the skills and giving responsibilities. These are the people that will make your dream reality.

To enable them to do this you need to build the right resources around them, and build systems to support them in their work – ensuring that the right things are done in the right way.

Finally you need to protect everything you've built. Life never runs smoothly and your business needs to be ready for the challenges that will be thrown at it. Entrepreneurs develop plans and strategies for dealing with problems that give their businesses security.

Let's look at each of these in turn.

BUILDING A BRAND

This is instinctively the first thing that many small business owners and entrepreneurs turn to, except the former think it only means deciding on the company name and logo.

Highly successful entrepreneurs seem to understand in their bones that it's about embedding the company's focus and attitudes into every aspect of the business.

Yes, the name and logo need to represent these – but so does the way customer enquiries are dealt with, products or services are delivered, staff are treated, and every single aspect of what the business does.

As the leader you need to exemplify the company focus and attitudes. The leader of Disney can't go around swearing, looking miserable and hating kids. The leader of Google can't find computers boring and not know how to use the Internet. You have to be an ambassador for your company – and a living example of everything it stands for.

So what does your company stand for? If that's a difficult question then you need to spend some time on this. Work back through Chapter 3 on Focus to develop a clear purpose for the business.

The next step is to develop the company attitude.

Company attitude

In the very first chapter we heard how important it is for you to develop and practise the right attitudes in order to achieve entrepreneurial success.

The same is true of the business as a whole. In order to achieve its focus, the company will need to develop a set of core attitudes that everyone will exemplify.

If you were starting Disney for example (whose focus is 'To make people happy'), you would perhaps decide that the important attitudes for the company to embody are of being: fun, family friendly, and creative.

These attitudes would then need to be embedded in everything the company does – from the stationery to the product or service, and even including the way it works behind the scenes. For example, you might start a company playgroup on the premises to enable parents to have their children nearby, knowing that they are well looked after.

What are the right attitudes for your company to have?

Build them into people's Talent Cakes, and demonstrate them in everything you do in your company – from the letterhead to your products.

The company focus and the company attitude are the essence of your brand, and the visual identity you adopt for it should reflect them. But remember that the brand goes well beyond this: everything your company does communicates something about it. Make sure it's the right message.

BUILDING A TEAM

It seems almost too obvious to state: the difference between your business being a one-man-band and a fast-growth entrepreneurial business is your team.

If your business depends too much on you, it will be very limited indeed.

So what are the elements of a successful entrepreneurial team? I like to use the analogy of the crew of a plane, as follows.

Pilot (the entrepreneur)

This is you. You're in charge. That means you generally don't do most of the technical job of actually operating the plane, because that is handled by your co-pilot and the rest of the flight crew, but you've set the destination and you have overall responsibility for everything to do with the plane. If the plane is only small, with a smaller crew, then you will be more involved – but if it's a big plane your role is to lead the others rather than dish out peanuts.

Flight crew (management team)

These are the very few people (between one and five, depending on the size of the company) who form the top management team in the business. They're with you up in the cockpit (except the one who's in charge of the cabin crew, who works with them but maintains close contact with the flight deck), and undertake the main duties of flying the plane, such as navigation, engineering, communications, operating the controls, and co-ordinating the cabin crew, ground support staff and air traffic control. They represent each key area of activity in the business, and report to you. Often some of them will be co-founders of the business with you, or will have joined in the early days.

They will be your trusted advisers, your confidants. They should all have a complete and frank understanding of everything within the business. These people take a role in general management as well as responsibility for their specialist area. You're likely to want one of them to focus on customers and sales, one to focus on the operations side of the business – doing whatever it is you do, and one to focus on the behind-the-scenes nuts and bolts of running the company, such as money and legal issues. As the business grows you may decide to expand this team, or you may decide to keep it small on purpose for better communication and trust. If you have less than three flight crew in the early days, you will have to split the roles between you.

Here's the crunch: after the sensitive first few years, the flight crew should be capable of running the business without you. You've seen the air disaster movies where the pilot gets food poisoning or has a heart attack – how would your flight crew cope? Would your plane crash, or would they complete the journey safely?

In the very early stages of the business this scenario is obviously difficult to contemplate, as you'll still have a crucial role. But as the business grows you should add to the core team, and develop their skills and capabilities, with the idea in mind that they run the business, gradually taking over from you.

Cabin crew (staff)

These are the people who fly with you, dealing mostly with serving the customers and doing the day-to-day work. They get people on the plane, look after them in-flight and generally take care of any front-of-house duties. They liaise with the flight crew to get instructions and to feed back any important information.

The cabin crew will probably join your company once it has been through its first stages of growth, and won't be as closely involved with it as your flight crew. It's vital that you pick people with the right attitude, and then inspire them with your vision and enthusiasm – because these are the people your customers will see. To them, these people *are* your business.

I found a distinct difference in how these people were recruited and managed between small businesses (that have always stayed small despite the owners' ambitions) and entrepreneurial companies that grow rapidly.

The difference was that the small business owners surround these people with rules about what they can't do, and check and monitor them. The entrepreneurs chose people with the right attitude in the first place, then gave them a clear focus and set of responsibilities. They created systems to help them deal with repetitive tasks quickly and easily, allowing the team members to focus on what was really important – and allowing them to exercise their judgement and creativity to create more fulfilling work.

One company had a policy that its customer service team could do anything, at any cost, that they thought was the right and fair way to resolve the problem for the customer. The only criterion the staff had to consider was 'Do I think this is the right thing to do?' In other companies they would be 'empowered' to 'refund up to £30 without referring up to a supervisor' or 'send a discount voucher for a future purchase', leaving the customer annoyed and the staff member feeling powerless and trapped between management and client.

What difference did this make to the company? Did they go bust under the huge flood of expensive decisions that their customer service team made? Nope. They increased their staff retention rate enormously, because the team members were happy and felt they were doing more fulfilling work, plus they didn't have such frustrated customers battling the system to get a fair solution, in fact they got lots of nice letters and calls of gratitude. They also increased the customer retention, and they gained many more referrals from existing customers, so sales went up too.

Entrepreneurs realize that most people are good people. If you are clear about your expectations in terms of focus, attitudes and responsibilities, then they will do their very best to deliver. They start by trusting people, but come down like a ton of bricks on those who breach this trust. Small business owners start by distrusting people, making them earn the trust, but always being wary. This creates a 'them and us' culture in the business, and massively reduces the effectiveness and involvement of your team.

The final challenge is to resist meddling. When you're watching your cabin crew doing their work you might notice that they do some things differently. That doesn't mean they're doing it wrong. In fact this is the equivalent of evolution in nature. Some of these differences won't work and will die out – but others will work really well and will be picked up by others, creating a better end result. The world outside is changing, and so should your ways of working. Your job is to set the direction that you're all going in, not give turn by turn instructions. Let them work out the detail themselves, and just support them with advice and training when required.

Trust people, make your expectations clear, enthuse them, support them, stand back, and watch the magic of a great team at work. You'll be amazed what can be achieved.

Ground support staff (funders and suppliers)

Every plane needs suppliers on the ground to deal with specialist jobs like loading the luggage, conducting security checks, maintaining the plane, and even providing the bags of peanuts! It also needs to be filled with enough fuel to make the journey.

Your business is just the same. You need funders to fuel your business with money. You need suppliers to provide you with goods and services to enable you to do what you do for your customers.

You'll reap the rewards if you involve these people and organizations as much as possible in the team. Let them know exactly where the business is going, keep them up to date with how you're doing. Treat them like your cabin crew: make your expectations very clear in terms of *their* focus, attitudes, skills and responsibilities.

Build up a relationship between each supplier and at least two members of your flight or cabin crew. Establish trust, openness and standards. Monitor the relationship to clarify that your expectations are being met, and reward good suppliers with loyalty and praise. Give suppliers the opportunity to put mistakes right – they're only human too – but change those that keep letting you down. Your passengers come first.

Develop a process for assessing potential new suppliers. Get references, get samples of the products or try out the services. Check industry news and gossip. Negotiate and agree prices and other important factors in advance – in writing. If necessary draw up a contract. Always read any contract they present you with, and get legal advice if you don't understand anything, are concerned about clauses, or if it's an important contract.

With your funders it's especially important to build a close relationship. They supply you with the money (or fuel) you need to keep your business going. They could be a bank, private investor, asset finance provider, or a range of other financial organizations – but their expectations are the same. They want to know how you're doing, and silence worries them. Worst of all, they hate surprises.

If you keep them up to date, they'll be much more prepared to help you out if problems arise.

A skill of entrepreneurs is making their funders and suppliers proud to be associated with the business. You need to get them as passionate about what you do as your crew.

Air traffic control (advisers)

Small businesses that stay small avoid using outside expertise. They think they're saving money.

Entrepreneurs know that good advice is an investment, and surround themselves with experts in different fields. A great accountant, a smart lawyer (perhaps a couple in different fields, such as intellectual property, commercial property, employment law, etc), selected consultants who can add real value, and others.

The key is in finding the right advisers. They must be genuine experts in their field, and earn your trust and confidence. If that's not the kind of adviser you have, change them!

Things to bear in mind when selecting advisers:

1. Do they have the right professional qualifications, memberships of professional bodies, etc?

2. Are they well respected by their fellow professionals?

3. Do they know about your industry?

4. Can you speak to other clients of theirs with similar businesses?

5. Do they listen to you enough, or do they just talk at you?

6. Are they interested in you and your business?

7. Do they understand what the issues are?

8. Do you like them? This question surprises a lot of people, but it is important as you'll be working with your advisers a lot. You don't have to become best buddies, but a friendly professional relationship is important. If you think they are annoying or too self-obsessed then you're unlikely to want to seek their counsel at the appropriate times. Trust your gut instincts.

9. How much is it going to cost?! Check this at a very early stage. What happens if it ends up taking longer than they thought?

There are some great advisers out there, there are good-enough advisers – and there are bad ones. I had a terrible experience with an accountant.

He would charge for work he hadn't done, including one invoice for filling in some official forms that were in my handwriting! I had been naïve and trusted him simply because of his professional qualification. I've learned my lesson and now check out my advisers carefully, and agree fees, etc well in advance.

Advisers don't just have to be for the formal stuff – legal and financial issues and so on – the right ones can also help you develop your skills as an entrepreneur and leader, and help you and your colleagues develop key areas of the business, such as sales and customer service.

This is where a mentor can be really helpful. This is someone you admire and trust, and who probably has some experience in building or running a business, rather than a professional qualification.

'Real world' experience is difficult to find from any other route, so I highly recommend that you seek out someone to mentor you in this way. But, from the questions I'm asked at seminars I give, a lot of people find this difficult. Here are some suggestions to help you find a mentor:

1. Do you have family members, or friends of the family, who have started or managed a business?

2. Do you know anyone locally who has set up their own business, or who manages a business?

3. Is there anyone in your industry who has experience that could be useful to you?

These are all good places to start. Even if these people can't help themselves, they'll probably know someone who can.

With your mentor and your professional advisers, you will have a great air traffic control team, who can help guide you and your crew in a successful flight, keeping you safe and on course.

BUILDING RESOURCES

Entrepreneurs are masters at gathering resources. That could be anything, depending on what line of business you're in.

But building your resources doesn't mean spending lots of money. The real entrepreneurs beg, borrow, haggle, and buy secondhand. They get creative and use resources for new purposes. They get adventurous and try new things.

The end result is that their companies are well equipped with the essentials in a sensible way, and at sensible prices.

The dot.com boom and bust companies went crazy on resources, buying new, buying top-of-the-range, and even buying stuff they didn't need at all because it was 'cool'.

I hate to hark on about Gordon Ramsay's 'Kitchen Nightmares' TV programme, but it contained so many useful business lessons. One week he went to sort out a small Italian restaurant in an English town. The young chef had bought the restaurant to start the business of his dreams, which was now struggling and about to go bust. The equipment in the kitchen was all a bit shoddy – and all very dirty – but he had a flashy new BMW outside, with a personalized number-plate!! He'd bought it when he started the business, because his image was more important to him than the reality behind the scenes.

True entrepreneurs don't do anything like this, in fact I know some won't splash out that much just on a car even now!

Remember the rich/poor attitude from the first chapter. You don't have to spend a lot of money, just be clever about how you spend it.

Buy things on auction websites, find out about secondhand dealers in your industry or general ones for office furniture, etc, and always haggle to try to get a better deal when you do have to buy new.

But don't let being careful with money mean you waste a lot of time. Buy on value rather than simply on price. A cheap machine that keeps breaking down and wasting the time of your team members is worse than a more expensive one that works.

As the leader it's your responsibility to ensure that your team have the resources they need to do the job. You can delegate this to key individuals with clear guidelines and budgets, but it's important to keep an eye on it and ensure that people aren't struggling with a computer that crashes all the time and drives them nuts. Take out the stress, and provide the proper tools for the job.

You also need to keep one step ahead. What are the resources that your team will need in the near future?

BUILDING SYSTEMS

People setting out on their entrepreneurial journey reel away from the words 'systems' and 'procedures'. They may have worked in big companies where those words mean lack of freedom, stupid rules and worse. But the successful ones seem to instinctively build systems into their businesses, even though they may not even recognize it themselves.

The fact is that entrepreneurial businesses have to be so much more efficient than other companies. They are growing so fast, and with less money behind them than bigger ventures so time and resources have to be used as carefully as possible.

At the same time these businesses realize that one thing that turns customers on is reliability. Customers don't actually want their expectations to be exceeded (otherwise that would be a new set of expectations, and we'd all get really confused), they just want them to be met. This is very rare: think of your own experiences with companies you deal with.

So, you need to conserve time and resources, and your customers want things to be predictable and reliable. You need systems to help with this.

These systems mean that everyone wins. A common objection is that having systems restricts the entrepreneur or their staff in how the job is done, but it doesn't. It just makes the repetitive jobs easier, allowing more time and resources to be focused on the new and exciting. Once you've experienced this, you'll be hooked on systems!

What jobs do you and your team have to do repeatedly? The next time you do them, develop a system so they're easier in the future.

What's in a system?

The system you design will have a step-by-step list of the actions needed (a checklist), and then it might also have:

1. Standard documents or document templates.

2. Responsibilities assigned to particular people.

3. Pre-prepared resources located in a particular place.

For example, you might find that you are regularly being asked by customers for a catalogue, price list and some samples. This can become one of those boring jobs that people just put off because they have to fiddle around collecting all the bits, write a letter, and so on. Worse, some members of your team might forget to include certain samples.

The system to make this easier and more reliable might be:

1. Give someone the responsibility of keeping a certain stock level of made-up sample packs. Have a box or other package that is perfect for this job, a list of which samples are to go in which pack, and sets of stickers to identify each type of pack, such as 'industrial widget samples', 'consumer widget samples', etc. Set aside a special place where these will be stored.

2. Develop a document template for a letter to send with the packs, and save it in a central place where anyone can access it.

3. Create a checklist of the steps that people need to take each time they receive a request to send a sample pack. You may want to attach this as a page two in the document template, so you know where it is, and it gets printed with the letter and can be ticked off as they complete each part of the task. You should also have a copy of each checklist in a file that anyone can access, or you may give a copy of such a file to everyone.

The checklist in this example might say:

1. Open the document template at Server/Letters/SendInfoPack.doc.

2. Edit the customer's name and address details.

3. Edit the section showing which sample packs are enclosed.

4. Add a personalized paragraph at the end of letter.

5. Check through letter for spelling and correct details.

6. Print two copies of the letter.

7. Put one copy of the letter in the sales diary file for 10 days away to allow follow up.

8. Go to section 'C' of the storeroom and get a catalogue box from the bottom shelf. Check it contains a catalogue and price list.

9. Get the appropriate sample packs from the second shelf.

10. Double check you have the right sample packs against what you have written in the letter!

11. Pack and seal the box on the packing table.

12. Fold the letter into quarters so that the address shows, and insert the letter into a clear adhesive pouch (to be found in the box on the packing table). Stick this on the parcel.

13. Place the parcel in the postbag next to the packing table.

14. Congratulations on getting us another potential customer!

Now, think how useful this system will be when you recruit new members of staff, when you have someone in on work experience, or when someone is on holiday and another member of the team is standing in for them. This task will still be done in the same way. It's reliable for the customer, time saving for you.

Obviously, the example I've chosen here is a very basic one, but the ideas can be applied very powerfully to the more involved and serious repetitive tasks that you and your team have to do.

Templates are great

Creating standard documents that can be quickly and easily used throughout your business is extremely beneficial, even where they don't need to be used within a full system. It saves time, and ensures that a professional and consistent image is presented to the outside world.

Here are some ideas for useful templates:

- Standard contracts for use with all customers.

- Purchase orders for placing orders with suppliers.

- Sales orders for customers to place orders with you.

- Directions to your company premises. It's great to just be able to attach this document to emails rather than have to type out directions each time when people are coming to visit.

- Fax header sheets.

- A word document that has lots of 'boiler-plate' paragraphs that need to be used in your company, so that people can cut and paste them into letters or emails. This could be a description of the company and your background, details of the benefits of your products or services, etc.

Pre-preparing resources

The simpler to use you can make everything, the better. This doesn't just go for making up sample packs and so on as mentioned above, it's about looking at the use of every resource and making it easier.

Insider Knowledge

One example of pre-preparing resources is an entrepreneur-run airline that was ordering a new fleet of passenger jets from a major manufacturer. They were given a tour round one of the fantastic new planes, and shown all the amazing new displays and controls for the crew. When they placed the order they set one condition: that everything on the plane be made to look like the old version of the plane. So where there was a fancy display screen it should be replaced with a simple series of display lights and so on. It could be as hi-tech as they liked behind the scenes, but it must look and operate just like the older planes. The reason for this was that the airline wanted every single plane in its fleet – no matter how old or new – to be exactly the same, so that all pilots could fly all planes, and all crew could

▶

work on all planes. This gave them the flexibility and reliability that they needed. They pre-prepared the resources to save problems with training or staff rosters.

Get into a systems-building mode. Whenever you or your team are doing a job that is repetitive, create a system for it – and build new reliability and speed into your business.

BUILDING SECURITY

Building all of the above for your business is hard enough, but you also have to be aware that problems can occur, competitors may try to sink you, the economy might change, and any of a seemingly endless number of hazards may present themselves.

As the leader in charge of building the business, you need to equip it with systems that provide some kind of security against this. You need to prepare for problems and be ready to respond.

RADAR

You and your flight crew need to be constantly scanning the skies for any potential hazards. The first step is to work out where those challenges could come from. They tend to fall into four areas:

Internal. Team members could fall out with each other, leave, hate their job, make a major mistake, or have an accident. You might run out of money, your bank could call in the overdraft, your IT network could go down, or any number of things could cause you problems inside the company.

Customers and sales. A customer might go out of business, they might have problems and pay you late, they might change supplier, the trends or fashions might change and put you out of favour, their needs might change and make your products out of date, your sales figures might be lower than expected, and so on. Of course you might get challenges from good things happening too. What if a major celebrity were photographed using your product and sales went through the roof – how would you cope with demand?

Competitors. Other companies aren't going to stand still why you try to make your business a success. They will try to undercut your prices, badmouth you, run major promotions, take your customers. And companies who aren't your competitors now – or don't even exist yet – could become your rivals. Where might they spring up from? What might they do?

Murphy's law. This is everything that is completely outside your control, but Murphy's law says if you don't want it to happen, it will. What could happen to annoy you? Laws could be introduced or changed, taxes could be increased or changed, the weather could be wrong, a bad news event could happen. This is the kind of scenario where you introduce a new ice cream range – and it turns out to be the coldest summer for 200 years, or you introduce an amazing new line of gadgets – and a new government trade deal is announced with some country in the Far East meaning that cheap copies will flood the market.

Insider Knowledge

The online airline ticket website, Opodo, had been preparing for months to launch its new business in a blaze of expensive marketing. Unfortunately the launch date was planned for 12 September 2001.

You can't prevent this sort of thing from happening, and there's no point complaining about it. Just predict it and prepare for it. It's far better to have back-up plans that rot away in your filing cabinet because the event never happened than have the business thrown into disaster because of a potential problem you missed.

To help identify threats to the business, and monitor them I've developed a simple tool called the RADAR.

Designing your RADAR

Draw a circle, with a big dot in the middle to represent your business. Divide the circle into four quarters. Label the quarters 'Internal', 'Customers and Sales', 'Competitors', and 'Murphy's law'.

For each quarter of the circle, spend some time brainstorming problems that could affect your business. The more likely they are to happen, or the more dangerous they would be to you, the nearer to the centre they go. If they're unlikely, a long time in the future, or not very serious, they can go further out to the edge. You may need to put numbers in little circles on the RADAR itself and do a corresponding numbered list down the side – or you can just draw the RADAR on a really big whiteboard or huge sheet of paper.

It's best to involve your flight crew in this, and perhaps explain how the exercise is going to work at one management meeting. Ask everyone to go away and develop their own RADARS which they will present to the next meeting, building up an overall company RADAR from the combined results. There is likely to be some discussion about what's a real risk and what isn't – but if in doubt it's far better to have it on the RADAR than leave it off, and if there's any argument about how close to the centre it should go, be biased towards putting it at the estimate that's the closest to the centre. Be pessimistic when doing RADAR planning.

Using your RADAR

Now you have this tool, it should be used at least once a quarter in management meetings, perhaps even more frequently in fast-growing companies or industries.

The first step is to review the risks on the RADAR already, and decide if there are any more that need to be added. Then ask these questions:

1. Are there any risks we need to take immediate action on?

2. Are there any risks we need to plan for now and be ready for?

3. Is there any preventative action we can take on any of these risks in advance of them happening?

4. Have any risks moved closer, i.e. become more serious or more likely, or moved to be sooner?

5. Have any risks moved further away, or even off the RADAR?

If you decide you need to develop a plan for a RADAR event, set someone on your flight crew the task of developing the plan and bringing it to a future meeting for improvement and approval. They will need to investigate the possible shape and severity of the threat, and explore all the options for dealing with it. This takes time and thought and can't effectively be done then and there in the meeting.

Remember – entrepreneurial businesses succeed not because nothing bad ever happens to them, but because they are resilient enough to cope with the problems. They have a Plan B, and they never give up. The RADAR can help you prepare your Plan B's.

Intelligence gathering

To keep the radar working effectively you need to gather intelligence in each quarter of the circle. Delegate the responsibility for this, and ensure that people know how to find the information, and that others know how to pass it to them.

You can find useful information from many sources, including:

1. Websites: industry news sites, competitors' sites, suppliers' sites, customers' sites.

2. Internet search engines.

3. Trade press.

4. Business press.

5. General news press.

6. Gossip – this can be very important. Make sure your team have their ear to the ground and feed information back to the RADAR co-ordinators.

Financial planning

A major route to greater security for your business is ensuring you have enough cash. You and your flight crew should always know the cash position of the business now, and the forecast position each week for the next few months.

Running out of cash is the worst thing that can happen to a business, and all it takes to happen is a major customer refusing to pay, a bank calling in an overdraft, a sudden drop in sales, or an expensive unexpected problem.

This is one of the possible threats on the RADAR that is so serious you need to have a plan to tackle it. First, you need to develop an early warning system. The best way to do this is to monitor the stages of the sales process. Understand how each stage feeds into the next – 'If we get twenty new prospects, we end up preparing five quotations, and getting two sales', for example.

Then you can monitor the number of new prospects through the system, that enough of these are requesting quotes, and the right proportion of these are converting to sales.

If you're suddenly finding only five new prospects in a month, you know there's trouble coming further down the line, and you can take quick action. Or if you find that out of a hundred prospects you only ended up with four sales, you'll also know that something is going wrong and you can fix it.

Keep an eye on these early measurements and you can catch problems before they hit your cash flow.

It's also important to develop budgets: they don't need to be big doorstops, just an outline of income and expenditure under key headings.

Then you and your flight crew should regularly review the performance of the business at a monthly meeting. How did you do against budget? How is the cash flow?

The figures are guaranteed to be different to budget, but the key thing is to understand why. Why aren't as many customers taking out service contracts at the time of purchase as we predicted? Why are more people in Andy's region buying the top of the range widget than anywhere else? Why is this customer paying late?

Finding out why may help to find the root cause of the problem, and then you can fix it.

6

CHAPTER SIX
The sixth secret: Communication

The first thing to understand about communication is that everything you do says something about you and your business. Even not communicating anything says something.

So when entrepreneurs get communications right they're doing much more than issuing press releases or email newsletters – they're creating contact with their target audiences in a multitude of ways, involving people in the work of the company, building loyalty, and much more.

THE IMPORTANCE OF GREAT COMMUNICATION

Entrepreneurs do not realize their full potential single-handed. Their skill is in marshalling teams of people to do more together than anyone thought was possible. They sell this team on a grand vision – a focus – and inspire them to reach it. This is all about communication.

As an entrepreneur, any time you spend on your own is not the best use of your scarcest resource. There is only one of you, and you should not spend much of your time in a room on your own doing paperwork or writing reports. When an entrepreneur is on their own, they're just administering a business, not leading it.

So far you've developed the attitudes and focus. You've spotted the opportunity and developed the talent to take advantage of it. Then you've been building a lasting successful business around this.

What underpins all of this, and is vital in every one of those steps, is communication.

As the entrepreneur, you have two communications roles: leader and ambassador.

Leader

This is the role your team see you in. You set the direction for the organization, and you keep everyone on track. This means celebrating, rewarding and disciplining where appropriate. It also means being an example, rather than simply preaching from on high.

The way you act communicates far, far more to your team than what you say about how they should act.

They want to look up to you and respect you. They need an authority figure who they have confidence in to make the key decisions and steer them in the right direction. Nobody likes being in an aimless, drifting organization.

That involves communication. Regularly and clearly communicate your vision for the future and what the organization exists for. Be absolutely clear about the attitudes you expect.

You can't just assume people 'get it' first time, or that they'll always remember it. You need to constantly, and consistently, reinforce the message.

To communicate in your leadership role, bear in mind the following:

- **Meetings.** You need to become an expert at leading meetings. This begins with the objective, a clear agenda, then a well-chaired meeting, followed up afterwards by action-based minutes, and then a later follow-up on those action points. To chair effectively be firm on timings and topics, fair in terms of who gets to speak and for how long and, the secret golden rule of chairing – you're only allowed to ask questions. When you're in control it's too easy to make statements and guide the meeting. You should be enabling the group, not lecturing them. If you think something's a bad idea, don't say so, ask for an explanation of how it would work, or what could go wrong.

- **Your mood.** The way you seem to feel when you walk into work in the morning will affect everybody else in the building. If you seem depressed people will worry. If you're excited they'll be excited. Think about this before you walk in each day.

- **Your treatment of others.** This sets the tone for the company, so show respect, be interested, be calm and generally treat everybody the way you want them to treat everybody else.

Ambassador

This is your role in the outside world. You are the top representative of your company to funders, suppliers, prospects, customers, government, the local community, the media and the general public.

Your team may find it useful to 'wheel you in' to meet and greet new or potential customers, host a dinner, give a speech at an event, and so on. Don't make the mistake of thinking that this kind of activity isn't useful. Ten minutes of interested attention from the company founder can be enough to swing an order from a new customer, or to cement the relationship with an existing one.

Your role as ambassador is a great way to spend your time, but don't let any one appointment suck up too much unless it's really important. Your team should be handling the majority of the relationships, and your role is more ceremonial.

The ambassador's role also involves meeting new people and introducing them to the company in the correct way. You might be at a business dinner and meet a potential new customer. Make sure that the connection is made between them and the correct member of your team, and then follow up with the team member later to find out how it's going.

Here are some tips for being a great ambassador:

- Listen to each person you meet as if they are the most important thing in your world for that time. Do not check your mobile phone as they talk, glance over their shoulder, and so on. Look them in the eye and listen carefully.

- Learn how to ask good questions. Be really curious and interested in the people you meet. Be seen to be keen to know more.

- Practise remembering people's names. You can learn this skill. The first step is to actually listen to their name when they introduce themselves. Repeat it immediately while looking at their face, so you link the name and the face in your mind: 'Hello Fred, pleased to meet you.' Then use their name regularly during the conversation. Then you just have to trust your brain and use the first name that pops into your head when you meet people. You'll be amazed to be right most of the time, and be ready to laugh it off on the few occasions it doesn't work!

- Listen more than you talk.

- Learn how to bring conversations to a polite but firm end when the time is right.

- Practise introducing yourself in a concise but interesting way that clearly explains who you are and what your company does.

- Learn to be self-aware, and catch yourself being boring, overbearing, and exhibiting other undesirable traits.

- Don't put up with other people's undesirable traits. Move the conversation on, or end it – politely but firmly.

- Be there to give rather than to take. Who can you help and how?

- Set an objective for each occasion beforehand. It could be to get to speak to a particular person, to cement an existing relationship, or anything else. Be clear about what matters to you, and make sure you achieve it.

- Always have business cards to hand.

- Make notes of every action item that results from every person you meet. This could be on the back of their business card, or in a notebook you carry for the purpose. Follow up on this as soon as you are back in the office.

Your target audiences for your ambassador's role, along with the communications they want from your company, and therefore you, include:

- **Funders.** These people want to know that their money is safe, and that they will earn a good return. They will want regular updates, and an honest assessment of progress. They hate surprises.

- **Suppliers.** These people will want to know that it's safe to do business with you, but you will also get better service if you can enthuse them with what your company does and its prospects.

- **Customers.** These people want to know that it's safe to do business with you, and that your products and services will meet their needs and expectations. They will want a consistent message of what it is your company stands for – and they will want the reality to measure up.

- **Your prospects.** Much the same as with customers, except that these people don't know much about you yet. You have to work harder with them.

- **The public.** As you grow your local community will take more of an interest in you, and if you build a well-known brand then the general public will be a target audience for you.

- **The media.** To reach many of your other target audiences you'll need to go through journalists. It will really benefit you to think of these people as a separate audience.

- **The industry.** Depending on your line of business it might be important to you to communicate to others in your industry. This can help you find good new suppliers, sign up new customers, and keep one over on the competition. The more you build your reputation, the easier it will be to do business.

FOCUS AND ATTITUDE

As ever, it's all about focus and attitude. You know what your company focus is, and you know what your company attitudes are, and all your communications should not only be consistent with these, they should strongly demonstrate them. Every communication, full stop.

Have you ever seen Michael O'Leary of Ryanair giving any kind of quote to the media that is not about being low cost?

Every letter that leaves your building, every email, every press release, every page on your website, every speech you give to staff or the public, every advertisement, your packaging, your carrier bags, your till receipts, your invoices, your envelopes, your vehicles, and every other form of contact your company has with anybody at all is a communication, and should reflect and reinforce your focus and attitudes.

Insider Knowledge

Virgin is always friendly, emphasizing customer service and value, but a bit cheeky in poking fun at bigger competitors. Test them out. Try some of their products, visit the website, write to them, ring them up. How do they measure up? Pick a few other entrepreneurial companies that you respect. Browse their websites, visit their premises, pick up their marketing materials, look at their products. What is their style of communication? Is it consistent? Does it fit well with their brand?

This standard of communication is a really, really hard commitment to live up to. Everybody has off days, there'll be times that it slips (as it does even with Virgin and all these other companies we hold in high regard), but the aim is always 100 per cent. Don't settle for less.

WALK THE TALK

It's not enough to just say the right things to communicate your message. You also have to do the right things. Remember the maxim 'actions speak louder than words'. Don't just say you think that keeping the costs low in the business is important – refuse to take a company car, fly economy, get a cheap, secondhand desk or don't go out for fancy lunches.

Insider Knowledge

When he started Amazon, Jeff Bezos wanted to communicate to everyone how important it was to keep costs down. Did he stand up and make a speech about it? Did he send a memo round? No – he needed a desk, and he made one out of an old door rather than go and buy one. That sent out a clear message about keeping costs low. After that it became a ritual for every new employee to build their own 'door desk'.

You know what your key messages are – how can you put them into action yourself to inspire others to do the same?

THE INVOLVEMENT LADDER

If you communicate effectively, you'll do more than simply get your message across – you'll actively increase the level of involvement of the person you're communicating with.

Entrepreneurs are great at this. Call it inspiration, motivation, salesmanship, or whatever you like, but the other person develops loyalty and a sense of belonging to the organization – and a belief in the focus, the cause. That leads to them working harder, buying more, or simply spreading the word.

The steps on the involvement ladder are shown below. In this discussion I'm focusing on customers, but the involvement ladder works in communications with any target audience.

Awareness

This is the bottom rung. To even get on the ladder people have to know that you exist. This tends to be the main, or even sole, focus of most people's marketing. They blow the whole budget on glossy ads, brochures, and so on, and then wonder why nothing much happens as a result. What they achieve is awareness, and that's simply basecamp, the first rung to start your next expedition from. You need to keep some resources in reserve to move these people up the involvement ladder, otherwise it's a wasted investment.

The most cost-effective and often the most generally effective forms of awareness are public relations, recommendations and product placement.

Public relations

A lot of entrepreneurs have become very good at gaining coverage in the media, whether that's the mainstream press or specialist trade press. Some use agencies to help them achieve this, but many do the necessary work in-house. To be successful in this you need to have a clear and interesting story about what your company focus is – why you exist – and also a different attitude to the norm. If you're setting up a new kind of bank and your focus is to maximize shareholder profit by maintaining the industry's high margins, and your attitude is cautious, businesslike and formal, then you're not going to get any coverage because that's not new, so it's not news. However, if you're on a mission to provide a better value bank with better customer service, and you're going to do this in a fun, perhaps cheeky, way – in the same way that Richard Branson challenged British Airways – then you'll get lots of coverage. That's news, and a lot of people will be interested. It's also a question of how many people in the target audience of the media outlet will be affected, or interested.

PR is about more than just sending out press releases. Try to be creative in the way you deal with the media.

Insider Knowledge

One entrepreneur I interviewed took samples of their (non-clothes-based but of interest to fashionable people) product to London Fashion Week and handed them out to the magazine editors. That got the business talked about, and a few journalists mentioned that they loved the product in their articles. This really started to build an interest in them and they found other journalists started writing about them too.

Recommendations

If you can encourage existing customers to recommend you to their friends or colleagues then you are raising awareness in a very effective way. Can you provide discount vouchers for your customers to give to friends?

Insider Knowledge

When Fred DeLuca started the Subway sandwich chain, he knew the power of word-of-mouth. When he opened a new store he would hand out vouchers that said 'Bring a friend and get 2 sandwiches for the price of 1' around the local area, and to customers who came into the store.

To be recommended you have to first make sure that you are meeting the expectations of your customers, then suggest the idea of telling their friends, and perhaps even provide some tools to help them do this, or rewards.

Product placement

A great way to make people aware of your products is to place them where your target audience is likely to be.

Insider Knowledge

Molton Brown, the luxury soaps company, provides its products at special rates to the right kind of restaurants and hotels. Customers in these places then get to try the product and often come to love it. That creates an awareness that would have cost a fortune if they had to pay to enclose sample packs in women's magazines. I know people who have bought Molton Brown products as a direct result of trying them in restaurants. It works.

Where do your target customers go? Is there a way of demonstrating your products or services there?

Contact

The next stage is contact. This could be a customer deciding to visit one of your shops, telephoning you, visiting your website, returning a reply card, or any other form of contact.

If you make the contact, then you might have to tackle the awareness rung first, and then try to tackle this rung.

Are you ready to deal with this contact? What will happen when the customer makes this contact? Are you and your team poised to move them up to the next rung on the ladder?

Contacts are so often dealt with badly. Think of the times that you've walked into shops and either been ignored or harassed. Think of the times you've spent on hold trying to telephone a company that you want to pay money to. Does this happen in your business?

Streamline your methods of communication for customers to make contact.

Two-way communication

This is when business really starts to happen. You and the customer are talking to each other, and listening to each other.

The problem with communication for most people is that they get stuck in 'transmit' mode. Some learn from experience or training to let go of the transmit button after a while and do some receiving – but they generally don't listen too well as they're focused too much on what they'll do when they next transmit.

When they start out, some entrepreneurs seem to make the mistake of thinking that communication is a one-way process – they have to tell people about themselves – but it's important to remember that it's actually a two-way process.

Listening is key. To build your business you need to encourage and enable communication from each of your audiences. How can you get them to tell you more about themselves, and the problems they need solutions to?

That knowledge will help you get way ahead of the competition.

Relationships

When you actually do business with someone then you are on this level of involvement. There is some kind of relationship there.

You each know about the other, there is a level of understanding, and there is a transactional relationship.

But like romantic relationships, it's fragile and a lot of careful nurture is required to keep it going. One bad mistake and it will damage trust.

You need to put a lot of effort and consideration into the relationship to move it to the next level.

Partnerships

This is where solid, mutual trust and respect have been established. There is security in a partnership. You have each proved yourself to each other, and you each like what you've seen. You're both open about what's on your mind. You're in it for the long term.

When you're at this stage with a customer you'll get the inside track on their plans for the future, you'll have easy access to them, and you can find out more details about the problems or aspirations they want you to help with.

This is a fantastic stage to get to with a customer, because it becomes less about sales, and more about simply helping them.

Community

The really clever entrepreneurs move to the next level, creating a community around their company – and often also use the community to help them achieve all the steps on the ladder!

This isn't just a communication between two individuals: many people who have a connection to your business speak to each other too and the network becomes like a spider's web.

Insider Knowledge

The Lush cosmetics company has online forums where its customers can chat to each other, and to staff, about the products and shops. Google has created online forums for webmasters who use its services on their websites to swap ideas and experiences.

Specialist shops have events and clubs to build communities around their outlets. Cycle shops run cycling clubs with organized rides and social meetings, hiking equipment shops organize guided treks, and restaurants organize wine and food tasting events.

Some people worry that if they create a community people will conspire to cut them out of the deal in some way, or will say bad things about them. In reality what happens is that your most loyal customers join the community, and are bound closer to you as a result. You become the hub.

This makes it hard for other companies to compete with you, because they can't create a similar community overnight. Customers will be reluctant to switch supplier because they'll lose the community, but the sense of community also makes them feel genuinely more loyal.

What do communities do? They share knowledge, ideas and contacts. They allow people to ask for help with particular problems, with the rest of the community providing answers. They provide product support. In fact, anything the members want.

Communities do need some work to get started, but after that they run themselves, with only a little input from you to guide things.

How can you build a community around your business?

ALWAYS ON

Clever entrepreneurs remember that everything is a communication, and use this to their advantage. Take a look at the bottles that Innocent fruit smoothies come in. Read the label, then look for the hidden messages under the bottle. They are creative, and very much reinforce their brand.

So start with things you already do. How can you use those to communicate with customers? Your products, bags, business cards, letterheads, invoices, etc.

Insider Knowledge

In one of my businesses we have developed our letterhead to include some tear-off coupons down the side, so that we can print special offers and order forms on them when we print the letters. We can tailor these offers to the addressee – and also have all their details already filled in on the order form when we mailmerge the letter!

Then start to look at new ways in which you can communicate.

7

CHAPTER SEVEN
The end?
The beginning?

So now you have an insight into the six secrets of self-made success, showing you how to be an entrepreneur.

We've looked at:

1. **Attitude**. The building block on which everything else rests. The six main attitudes of successful entrepreneurs are: Responsible, Principled, Open, Passionate, Versatile and Resilient. We looked at some ways to practise and develop these attitudes.

2. **Opportunity**. How to find or make opportunities in your business, at all stages.

3. **Focus**. How to develop a company focus, and how to keep it. Plus how to develop personal focus to be more effective.

4. **Talent**. How to develop a system for managing talent that is effective in an entrepreneurial business; why Attitude, Skills and Responsibilities are the key areas to focus on; and how it's important to keep developing your own talent.

5. **Building**. How entrepreneurs build lasting businesses rather than run around doing the day-to-day work. They build brands, teams, resources, systems and security.

6. **Communication**. How to craft consistent messages to different target audiences, and some tools to use. Also, how important it is to listen as well as talk – and how powerful communication can be in building a community around your business.

I hope you've found ideas to inspire you, and tools to help you out. But knowing this stuff is just the beginning – you need to put it into action. Why not take just one idea and try it out today?

That's the final difference between successful entrepreneurs and most people – they start. Most people talk or dream about what they could do, but never quite get round to making it happen. Entrepreneurs just get on with it.

What's next?

I recommend dipping into the book again from time to time to refresh your memory, or to find new inspiration relevant to your changed situation.

You can also join the online community to support this book, and my other books, at *www.flyingstartups.com*. It's a great way to meet other entrepreneurs and share experiences, ideas and tips. I'm also on the site regularly and look forward to meeting you there!

I wish you entrepreneurial success, and lots of fun along the way.

Steve

Index

HOW TO BE AN ENTREPRENEUR LIVE

The Six Secrets of Self-Made Success

By Steve Parks

Published by Red Audio

OUT NOW ON AUDIO CD

You can hear Steve Parks present his ideas on entrepreneurship live on stage to an audience of business owners.

Hear case studies and key ideas that will help you to develop the attitudes and focus of top entrepreneurs. Steve draws on in depth interviews with the highly successful founders of fast-growth businesses, and explains their beliefs and their systems.

This high energy, entertaining audio programme will inspire you to achieve success in your business.

You can buy the audio CD in all major bookshops, or online at
www.pearson-books.com

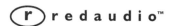

READY TO LAUNCH YOUR BUSINESS?

Get your business off to the best possible start with this definitive resource for entrepreneurs.

Start Up Business In a Box includes 3 of the UK's bestselling books for business owners and a sales training audio CD. This box set delivers essential advice, inspiration template resources, and masses of tips and techniques for launching your company. From developing your business idea and writing your business plan to officially requesting your company, securing funding, finding customers, recruiting staff and complying with key regulations, this box contains everything you need to start a business.

PLUS over £500 of exclusive discounts on all the essential products and services your new business will need.

Out now. Available from all good bookshops; or buy online at www.pearson-books.com

READ ON ...

Get your business off to the best possible start
with Steve Parks bestselling books for business owners
and entrepreneurs.

These guides deliver essential advice, inspiration, tips and techniques for
every stage in starting up and running your own business.

START YOUR BUSINESS WEEK BY WEEK

▶ 0273694472 ▶ £14.99

Want to start your own business but don't know where
to begin? Then overcome the challenges and turn your
ideas into reality in just six months with this definitive
week by week start up guide.

THE SMALL BUSINESS HANDBOOK

▶ 0273695312 ▶ £18.66

You have your business up and running but that's just
the beginning. This practical reference book is the
perfect guide to have by your side as you run and grow
your business. Filled with advice and guidance on all
the day-to-day aspects of running your enterprise, it
will ensure you are well equipped to tackle every new
situation that arises.

HOW TO FUND YOUR BUSINESS

▶ 0273695312 ▶ £14.99

This is THE book to take the pain out of financing your
start up! It provides the facts, figures and reassurances
you need to choose the right source of funding for you
and your business.

You can buy these books in all good bookshops, or online at
www.pearson-books.com

PEARSON
Prentice
Hall